PROPHETS, PRIESTS, AND KINGS

OLD TESTAMENT FIGURES WHO SYMBOLIZE CHRIST

ANDREW C. SKINNER

DESERET
BOOK

SALT LAKE CITY, UTAH

Library of Congress Cataloging-in-Publication Data

Skinner, Andrew C., 1951-
Prophets, priests, and kings : Old Testament figures who symbolize Christ / Andrew C. Skinner.
    p. cm.
Includes bibliographical references and index.
ISBN-10 1-57345-898-8 (hardbound : alk. paper)
ISBN-13 978-1-57345-898-6 (hardbound : alk. paper)
   1. Messiah—Biblical teaching.   2. Typology (Theology)   3. Bible.
O.T.—Criticism, interpretation, etc.   4. Church of Jesus Christ of
Latter-day Saints—Doctrines.   5. Mormon Church—Doctrines.   I. Title.
BS1199.M44.S55   2005
   221.6'4—dc22   2005027575

Printed in the United States of America
R. R. Donnelley and Sons, Crawfordsville, IN

10   9   8   7   6   5   4   3

CONTENTS

CONTENTS

CHAPTER 1

THE FIRST TESTAMENT OF JESUS CHRIST

Prophets of God orient us toward the most important things in life, and the most important things in life all center on the atonement of Jesus Christ. His redemptive sacrifice is the most important event in time or all eternity. A sure testimony of his redemption and resurrection is the most important possession we can acquire. A solemn promise to live as Jesus bids us is the most important commitment we can make. And the most important activity in which parents, siblings, friends, teachers, and leaders can engage is to help others come to Christ. President Gordon B. Hinckley summed up the matter in a most powerful and instructive way:

"With all of our doing, with all of our leading, with all of our teaching, the most important thing we can do for those whom we lead is to cultivate in their hearts a living, vital, vibrant testimony and knowledge of the Son of God, Jesus Christ, the redeemer of the world. . . . I would hope that in all we do we would somehow constantly nourish the testimony of our people concerning the Savior. I am satisfied—I know it's so—that whenever a man has a true witness in his heart of the living reality of the Lord Jesus Christ, all else will come together as it should. . . . That is the root from which all virtue springs among those who call themselves Latter-day Saints."[1]

The ultimate purpose of all scripture is the same as that of modern prophets—the witness of Jesus Christ and the bringing of souls to him. This is as true for the Old Testament as it is for the Book of Mormon or New Testament. In fact, in a literal way, the Old Testament is the foundation of both the Book of Mormon and the New Testament. All three books of scripture, the Old Testament, New Testament, and Book of Mormon, testify of the Messiah's mission, message, and manner. Sometimes we forget that the earthly Jesus regarded the Old Testament as the principal witness of his messianic role. "Search the scriptures," he said to the Jewish people in Jerusalem, "for in them ye think ye have eternal life: and they are they which testify of me" (John 5:39).

Jesus is actually being a bit reproving here, which would be easier for us to see if the "and" in this verse were read as "but." He is saying, in essence, "You study the scriptures because you think that activity brings eternal life, *but* the scriptures testify of *me,* and *I* give eternal life." In Jesus' day, the scriptures comprised the canonical books of the Old Testament, called the Torah. The Jewish sages of Jesus' day believed that the act of studying the Torah brought eternal life. This belief is confirmed in a statement by the great rabbi and contemporary of Jesus, Hillel, preserved in the Mishnah: "One who has acquired for himself Torah has acquired for himself the life of the world to come."[2] But Jesus pointedly taught that the scriptures did not bring salvation. Sacred writ was given to testify of him, and he, God, was *the* vehicle of salvation. It never was, and never will be, written words on a page that atone for sins: only the blood of the Messiah atones for sins. The scriptures do, however, bring earnest seekers to Jesus Christ and his doctrine.

The Old Testament testifies of Jehovah, the premortal Jesus Christ, and his unmatched power. It proclaims forcefully as well as subtly that the Lord's "mighty acts of deliverance anciently were types of . . . his ultimate act of deliverance, the Atonement."[3] The very concept of a redeemer is first and best exemplified for us in the Old Testament law of redemption, initially set forth in Leviticus 25. As first used in sacred writ, *redemption* "is a purely Hebrew word, belonging to the realm of family law, which denotes primarily the action of the next of kin to recover the forfeited property of a kinsman or to purchase his freedom if he has fallen into slavery."[4] Such is the essence of the Savior's work spiritually, and such is the way the Old Testament uses temporal matters to teach about spiritual, eternal matters.

Indeed, the Old Testament helps all of us to see that where the mortal life of Jesus Christ is concerned, everything about him had a foreshadowing, an ancient symbolic precursor, a specific likeness and similitude in earlier Israelite history. The Old Testament witnesses the coming of the earthly Messiah, the very same Being who ruled the universe as Jehovah before he took up his earthly tabernacle and was born as Jesus of Nazareth. The Old Testament demonstrates that the recorded actions of Jesus in the New Testament were a fulfillment of all the laws, ordinances, and institutions enacted in ancient Israel and that they revolved around the covenant God had made with his children.

In truth, the Hebrew term *berith,* which is translated as "testament," primarily means "covenant." That is to say, the Old Testament is really the Old Covenant, containing the laws, ordinances, sacrifices, symbols, and promises given to premeridian Israel by Jehovah, the premortal Christ. The New Covenant, or New Testament, documents the fulfillment of those laws, ordinances, sacrifices, symbols, and promises to ancient Israel with the coming of Jesus of Nazareth. The Old Covenant also describes ancient Israel's great apostasy, beginning at Mount Sinai, which led to the institution of the law of Moses. The New Covenant presents the new as well as restored laws, ordinances, sacrifices, symbols, and promises that constituted a new priesthood dispensation.

Thus, not only does the Old Covenant anticipate the New but the Old Covenant derives its name in relation to the New. No one described all of this better than the prophet Jeremiah:

"Behold, the days come, saith the Lord, that I will make a new covenant with the house of Israel, and with the house of Judah:

"Not according to the covenant that I made with their fathers in the day that I took them by the hand to bring them out of the land of Egypt; which my covenant they brake, although I was an husband unto them, saith the Lord:

"But this shall be the covenant that I will make with the house of Israel; after those days, saith the Lord, I will put my law in their inward parts, and write it in their hearts; and will be their God, and they shall be my people" (Jeremiah 31:31–33).

The Old Testament is the foundation not only of the New Testament but also of the Book of Mormon. The doctrine presented in the Book of Mormon is built upon the teachings of the brass plates, which may be thought of as a version of the Old Testament originating in the Northern Kingdom, just as our current Old Testament (King James Version) is a reflection of the Southern Kingdom, or Judean, version of the Old Testament record. The great Book of Mormon scholar Sidney B. Sperry said, "The Brass Plates may well have been the official scripture of the Ten Tribes."[5]

It will be remembered that after the death of King Solomon, the house of Israel (with its united twelve tribes) split into two kingdoms: the Northern Kingdom, also known as the Kingdom of Israel, or Ephraim, headquartered in Samaria; and the Southern Kingdom, or the Kingdom of Judah, headquartered in Jerusalem. Both kingdoms kept scriptural records that contained the same core teachings and prophetic books, including the five books of Moses, a history of God's dealings with ancient Israel, and the prophecies of many Old Testament prophets (1 Nephi 3:3, 20; 4:15–16; 5:11–14).

Lehi was of the lineage of the tribe of Joseph through Manasseh from the Northern Kingdom. He became custodian of the brass plates, a kind of Northern Kingdom version of the Old Testament, which included information about his forefathers (1 Nephi 3:3). The profundity of the Book of Mormon witness of Jesus as Messiah and Son of God is directly tied to the profundity of the Northern Kingdom version of the Old Testament in which it is grounded. The Book of Mormon is another testament of Jesus Christ (Title Page), and the brass plates contained many more of the testimonies, prophecies, and profound witnesses of the Messiah than did the Southern Kingdom version of the Old Testament with which the rest of the Christian world is familiar. The teachings of Zenock, Neum, and Zenos—prophets of the Old Testament era not preserved in our Southern Kingdom version—are truly magnificent in their messianic expressions (1 Nephi 19:10–21; Alma 33:14–17; 34:7; Helaman 8:18–20).

Given that the Old Testament is the foundational book for other scriptural records—records that have as their primary purpose to stand as testaments of Christ—it is fitting and accurate to characterize the Old Testament as the human family's first and foundational testament of the Lord Jesus Christ. Elder Bruce R. McConkie confirmed that assessment in these words:

"The Old Testament contains a revealed and abbreviated account of the creation of this earth, of man, and of all forms of life. It tells of the fall of man and of the Lord's dealings with Adam and the ancient patriarchs before the flood. It speaks of the Abrahamic and Israelitish covenants. A major portion tells how Israel became a nation, possessed their promised land, and, as the sheep of the Lord's pasture, were fed the prophetic word down through the ages. Included are poetical, prophetic, legalistic, doctrinal, didactical, and historical books. And, above all, interwoven through the whole account, from Adam to Malachi, is the promise of a Savior, a Redeemer, a Deliverer, a Messiah, a Suffering Servant, a Son of God, who would be born of woman, atone for the sins of the world, die and rise again in glorious immortality, and then return to that God whose Son and witness he was. The Old Testament is designed and prepared to teach the truths of salvation and to bear witness of the one who should come to redeem mankind and put into full operation all of the terms and conditions of the Father's great and eternal plan of salvation.

"As to the New Testament, it recounts the fulfillment of the ancient promises."[6]

In large measure, it was the contents of the Old Testament, the brass plates version, that the prophet Nephi was referring to when he exclaimed, "Behold, my soul delighteth in proving unto my people the truth of the coming of Christ; for, for this end hath the law of Moses been given; and all things which have been given of God from the beginning of the world, unto man, are the typifying of him" (2 Nephi 11:4).

The Hebrew and Aramaic word *Messiah* and the Greek word *Christ* (*christos*) mean "the anointed." When used as the title of an office, the terms refer to the Anointed One, the Deliverer-Redeemer-King whom the Jews were eagerly awaiting and who came to earth as Jesus of Nazareth. Jesus was the Anointed of the Father in our premortal existence to be his personal representative, to bring salvation to all of our Heavenly Father's children, to put into effect all of the terms and conditions of the Father's plan of exaltation. Thus, Peter says, "God anointed Jesus of Nazareth with the Holy Ghost and with power" (Acts 10:38).

Within the Old Testament, many types and shadows are to be found which point to the Messiah, our Savior, and his powers. As is the Lord's way, however, the most poignant and visible symbols of the Messiah were living symbols—those persons whose callings, speech, and actions mirrored Christ's, those who were themselves anointed in ancient Israel to perform their special duties in imitation of the Anointed One to come in the meridian of time, those whom we recognize as prophets, priests, and kings. Elder Bruce R. McConkie wrote: "No doubt there are many events in the lives of many prophets that set those righteous persons apart as types and shadows of their Messiah. It is wholesome and proper to look for similitudes of Christ everywhere and to use them repeatedly in keeping him and his laws uppermost in our minds."[7]

In ancient Israel, the three groups of people who were anointed to perform their responsibilities were prophets, priests, and kings. Prophets were anointed to their callings. The prophet Elisha, for example, was anointed prophet by his predecessor, Elijah (1 Kings 19:16). Priests were anointed to their office, as outlined in Exodus 40:15. Kings were anointed by the prophets (1 Samuel 10:1; 16:13; 2 Samuel 5:3; 1 Kings 1:39; 19:16; 2 Kings 9:3, 6; 11:12). These anointings were performed using olive oil, or olive oil mixed with spices, and represented Jesus Christ and his atonement.[8]

Jesus Christ, the Anointed One, of course, fulfilled all three roles of prophet, priest, and king, and even more. Thus, the very lives of Old Testament personalities—prophets, priests, and kings—are similitudes of the life of the great Prophet, Priest, and King, the Anointed One of the Father, the Holy One of Israel. In fact, it is about Jesus and all his precursors we sing when we give voice to the words, "He lives, and while he lives, I'll sing. He lives, *my* Prophet, Priest, and King."[9]

In this volume, we examine briefly a number of representative individuals whose lives and activities typified, paralleled, and foreshadowed the life and ministry of Jesus Christ, the great Prophet, Priest, and King of our profession (Hebrews 3:1). Our goal is to begin to see how the Old Testament testifies of the Savior in many ways and points us to him. If we hope to live up to the invitation proffered by President Howard W. Hunter "to live with ever-more attention to the life and example of the Lord Jesus Christ," we must begin to see all things bathed in the light of the Lord of life.[10] Such attention must start with the Old Testament—the human family's first testament of the Lord Jesus Christ.

CHAPTER 2

ADAM

OUR FIRST FATHER

Just as all things begin with Adam, whose fall was "father" to the Atonement, so, too, all foreshadowings, types, parallels, and imitations of the Messiah begin with the patriarch of the human family. Adam's first and most significant actions following his placement in Eden—his transgression and fall—are, ironically, a type and shadow of the atonement of Jesus Christ.

Usually most of us think of the fall of Adam in strictly negative terms and the atonement of Jesus Christ as having to make amends for the Fall. The Fall is the process by which humankind, the earth, and all life thereon became mortal. Before the Fall, there was no sin, no death, no procreation among any of the Lord's earthly creations. Adam and Eve possessed physical, but not mortal, bodies. After Adam and Eve partook of the forbidden fruit, all creation fell from God's presence, and all became subject to both physical and spiritual death. In emphasizing the severity of the mortal predicament inaugurated by the Fall, the brother of Jared exclaimed, "Because of the fall our natures have become evil continually" (Ether 3:2).

In truth, the Fall is very powerful—requiring an infinite

remedy, an infinite atonement. Viewed from another perspective, however, the fall of Adam paralleled and pointed to the atonement of Christ, and Adam himself paralleled and foreshadowed the person of Jesus Christ. Adam's fall gave mortal life, providing the way for all of our Heavenly Father's children who kept their first estate to receive a physical body (Abraham 3:26, 28). The atonement of Jesus Christ gives life yet again (after physical death) and provides a resurrected physical body for every soul initially given life through Adam (1 Corinthians 15:22). Thus, the actions of both Adam and Jesus Christ gave life to the entire human family, each in his proper order, and each inextricably linked to the other.

The apostle Paul discussed this similitude in two of his most significant theological discourses—his letters to the Corinthians and the Romans:

"And so it is written, The first man Adam was made a living soul; the last Adam [Christ] was made a quickening spirit. . . . And as we have borne the image of the earthy [man], we shall also bear the image of the heavenly [being]" (1 Corinthians 15:45–49).

"Death reigned from Adam to Moses, even over them that had not sinned after the similitude of Adam's transgression, who is the figure of him that was to come" (Romans 5:14).

The Hebrew word 'adam literally means "man" or "human," and Paul, a scholar of the Hebrew scriptures, or Old Testament, created a play on words to teach his readers the doctrine of our first father's similitude and typifying of Jesus Christ. Just as Christ is the "second" or "last" Adam (or man), so the reverse is also true: Adam, the first man, is the prefiguring of the second Adam, Jesus Christ. And just as every human is in the image of the first Adam, "the earthy," through birth, so every human will also bear the image of Jesus, "the heavenly," through resurrection.

Adam pointed to the coming of Jesus Christ in another way and in so doing paralleled the Savior's great gift to the human family. In Moses' restored introduction to the book we call Genesis, we are told of God's command to Adam to "offer the firstlings of their flocks, for an offering unto the Lord" (Moses 5:5). Adam was obedient for "many days" (in itself no insignificant lesson) before an angel of the Lord explained that these sacrifices were a similitude of the great and last sacrifice of the Only Begotten of the Father (Moses 5:7). So, right from the beginning, the life and mission of the Savior were foreshadowed. The Prophet Joseph Smith taught that Adam offered sacrifice as part of his priesthood responsibilities:

"The offering of sacrifice has ever been connected and forms a part of the duties of the Priesthood. It began with the Priesthood, and will be continued until after the coming of Christ, from generation to generation. We frequently have mention made of the offering of sacrifice by the servants of the Most High in ancient days, prior to the law of Moses; which ordinances will be continued when the Priesthood is restored with all its authority, power and blessings."[1]

In fact, Adam held the keys of the First Presidency and continued to hold those keys "from generation to generation."[2] But the priesthood he held was not called the Melchizedek Priesthood in his day. Rather, it was called "the Holy Priesthood, after the Order of the Son of God" (D&C 107:3). Adam, and all others following him until the time of Melchizedek, were explicitly designated as being "after the Order of the Son of God." An order is a systematic arrangement reflecting a pattern. Adam was explicitly designated as part of a pattern—the perfect pattern of Jesus Christ's life, his powers, actions, and sacrifice.

Thus, not only were Adam's sacrifices of animals a type, shadow, and similitude of the bodily sacrifice of Jesus Christ, but Adam himself was a similitude of the person of Jesus Christ. Under the ancient sacrificial system beginning with Adam, the animal chosen by the sacrificer represented, among other things, the one making the sacrifice. That is, the offering symbolically stood in place of the offerer. The offerer, through symbolic substitution of an animal, was giving himself completely to God. The sacrificer was making or declaring his life to be sacred or holy through the offering of a proxy. (Our English word *sacrifice* is a conjunction of two Latin words *sacer,* "sacred," and *facere,* "to make," and literally means "to make sacred.") In later Mosaic times, this transformation was graphically symbolized by the offerer's laying his hands on the living offering, prior to the actual act of sacrificing, to transfer personal sins and identity to the animal: "And it shall be accepted for [in behalf of] him to make atonement for him" (Leviticus 1:4). Thus, by offering sacrifice according to the will of God, Adam was acting as Jesus Christ would act—who offered sacrifice (the great and last sacrifice of himself) according to the will of God (JST Matthew 27:5). Adam was truly a likeness of him who was to come—Jesus Christ.

The same principle applies to all righteous persons in this last dispensation who offer profound sacrifice according to the will of God. They are similitudes or likenesses of Christ. There are many ways to offer this kind of sacrifice, but the sacrifice must follow the Lord's will and be rooted in a broken heart and contrite spirit. After his resurrection, Jesus told the Nephites that the nature of sacrifice had changed from animal bloodshed: "Ye shall offer up unto me no more the shedding of blood; yea, your sacrifices and your burnt offerings shall be done away. . . . And ye shall offer for a sacrifice unto me a broken heart and a contrite spirit" (3 Nephi 9:19–20).

A broken heart and a contrite spirit are a perfect likeness or similitude of Jesus' atoning experience, and he undoubtedly wants us to comprehend the nature of that atoning experience. The word *contrite* comes directly from a Latin root meaning "to grind." To be contrite is to be "crushed in spirit."[3] In Gethsemane, Jesus' spirit was crushed by the weight of the sins and sorrows of the world (he said he felt "very heavy," or weighed down; Mark 14:33). In Gethsemane, Jesus was ground and crushed like the olive (*Gethsemane* literally means "oil press"). And on Golgotha's cross, "Jesus died of a broken heart," the consequence of suffering for infinite sin and sorrow.[4]

Therefore, for us to offer a broken heart and a contrite spirit is to willingly repent, cultivate humility (eagerness to be taught) and meekness (poise in the face of provocation), and to patiently submit to *all* things that the Father sees fit to inflict upon us (Mosiah 3:19). It is to experience what Jesus experienced and yet to remain absolutely loyal to Deity, to serve with all of our might, mind, and strength. It is to suffer anguish, even godly sorrow, for our own sins—as much as it is possible for mortals to suffer—as well as feel pain for the sorrows of others. That is also called charity, or the pure love of Christ (Moroni 7:47). To experience what Jesus himself experienced is, by definition, a similitude.

There are other ways modern disciples symbolize, point to, and become types of Jesus Christ. One profound way for priesthood holders is to officiate in the ordinances of salvation. For example, Elder D. Todd Christofferson said, "In the baptism of a living person, the officiator acts, by proxy, in place of the Savior."[5] To stand in the place of the Savior is a sobering responsibility and a call for the highest level of behavior, true Christlike behavior, in our personal lives. Both brethren and sisters point to the life of Christ directly when they become Saviors on Mount Zion through searching out the names of deceased ancestors and performing the ordinances of salvation in their behalf in temples of the Lord. President Gordon B. Hinckley said: "I think that vicarious work for the dead more nearly approaches the vicarious sacrifice of the Savior Himself than any other work of which I know. It is given with love, without hope of compensation, or repayment or anything of the kind."[6]

All disciples of Jesus Christ, whether ancient or modern, are required to offer sacrifice in the similitude of the sacrifice of Jesus Christ, whether it was animal sacrifice *before* the resurrection of the Savior, or a broken heart and contrite spirit *after* the resurrection of the Savior. The reality of this doctrine was seen in vision by President Joseph F. Smith in October 1918: "And there were gathered together in one place an innumerable company of the spirits of the just, who had been faithful in the testimony of Jesus while they lived in mortality; and who had offered sacrifice in the similitude of the great sacrifice of the Son of God, and had suffered tribulation in their Redeemer's name" (D&C 138:12–13). All disciples of Jesus Christ, like Adam, must become likenesses of their Master, and their lives must point to him.

CHAPTER 3

ABEL, ENOCH, AND NOAH
OTHER FATHERS

A second antediluvian (pre-Flood) patriarch we must consider as a profound similitude of Jesus Christ is a person about whom the Judeo-Christian world knows very little. This is Adam's son Abel. Were it not for the added insights provided by the Joseph Smith Translation of the Bible, Abel would scarcely occupy anyone's attention except as an example of a tragic victim of sibling rivalry. With the blessing of restored texts through the gifts and powers of a modern prophet, however, we come to understand several important, even profound, concepts, including the following:

Abel offered sacrifice like his father, which was acceptable to the Lord and which pointed to the Messiah.

Abel's own death was truly a similitude of the death of Jesus Christ.

Abel was regarded by the people of Abraham's day as the one whose spilled blood redeemed them from their sins, rather than the spilled blood of the yet future Messiah and true Savior, Jesus of Nazareth.

15

First, the story of Abel's acceptable sacrifice is inextricably linked to his brother Cain. The scriptural record implies that from the time of his birth Abel gravitated to spiritual things and "hearkened unto the voice of the Lord" (Moses 5:17); Cain did not, saying: "Who is the Lord that I should know him?" (Moses 5:16). Like his father before him, Abel offered acceptable sacrifice to the Lord; Cain did not. The text of Moses tells us that the whole reason Cain offered a sacrifice in the first place was that Satan commanded him to do so: "And Cain loved Satan more than God. And Satan commanded him, saying: Make an offering unto the Lord" (Moses 5:18). Abel's sacrifice was a blood sacrifice of the firstlings of his flock, offered in faith and in the similitude of the blood sacrifice of the Son of God, Jesus Christ; Cain's sacrifice was the fruit of the ground, offered without faith, not in similitude of the Son, and not done immediately (Moses 5:19). Therefore, the Lord had respect for Abel's action but not for Cain's (Moses 5:20–21). The Prophet Joseph Smith elaborated on this point:

"By faith in this atonement or plan of redemption, Abel offered to God a sacrifice that was accepted, which was the firstlings of the flock. Cain offered of the fruit of the ground, and was not accepted, because he could not do it in faith, he could have no faith, or could not exercise faith contrary to the plan of heaven. It must be shedding the blood of the Only Begotten to atone for man; for this was the plan of redemption; and without the shedding of blood was no remission; and as the sacrifice was instituted for a type, by which man was to discern the great Sacrifice which God had prepared; to offer a sacrifice contrary to that, no faith could be exercised, because redemption was not purchased that way, nor the power of atonement instituted after that order; consequently Cain could

16

have no faith; and whatsoever is not of faith, is sin. But Abel offered an acceptable sacrifice, by which he obtained witness that he was righteous, God himself testifying of his gifts. Certainly, the shedding of the blood of a beast could be beneficial to no man, except it was done in imitation, or as a type, or explanation of what was to be offered through the gift of God Himself; and this performance done with an eye looking forward in faith on the power of that great Sacrifice for a remission of sins."[1]

Second, with regard to Abel's death as a similitude of Jesus' death, we know that Cain entered into a covenant with Satan, slew Abel, and shed his blood on the ground (Moses 5:32, 35). From a careful reading of Joseph Smith's translation of Genesis 5 (Moses 5) we know that Abel's death was premeditated murder, resulting from the conspiracy involving Satan and Cain. In fact, Abel was delivered by Satan into the hands of Cain, a very wicked man: "And Satan said unto Cain: Swear unto me by thy throat, and if thou tell it thou shalt die; and swear thy brethren by their heads, and by the living God, that they tell it not; for if they tell it, they shall surely die; and this that thy father may not know it; and this day I will deliver thy brother Abel into thine hands. And Satan sware unto Cain that he would do according to his commands. And all these things were done in secret" (Moses 5:29–30).

In parallel fashion to Abel's death, the death of Jesus Christ was also premeditated murder resulting from another horrible conspiracy. Jesus was delivered by Satan into the hands of wicked men through the treachery of one of Jesus' closest associates. The Gospel of Matthew identifies the original planners of the plot to murder Jesus as the chief priests, scribes, and elders of the people (Matthew 26:3–5). And the Gospel of Luke describes those sent to arrest Jesus as "the chief priests, and captains of the temple, and the elders" (Luke 22:52). But the agent of these conspirators, the grand conspirator and instrument of betrayal, was Judas Iscariot. The Gospel writers Luke and John are explicit in their testimony that Satan not only entered into a conspiracy with this member of the Quorum of the Twelve Apostles but he literally *entered* the body of the man (Luke 22:3; John 13:27). "Then entered Satan into Judas surnamed Iscariot, being of the number of the twelve. And he went his way, and communed with the chief priests and captains, how he might betray him unto them. And they were glad, and covenanted to give him money. And he promised, and sought opportunity to betray him unto them in the absence of the multitude" (Luke 22:3–6).

Just as Abel's death and ultimate sacrifice for righteousness' sake came from the shedding of his blood, so too Jesus' death and ultimate sacrifice resulted from the shedding of his blood. Truly, Abel's death was a similitude of the death of Jesus Christ.

The lost information that Abel was mistakenly identified as a redeemer or Messiah figure has been restored through Joseph Smith's inspired translation of Genesis 17. By the time of the patriarch Abraham, certain segments of the population had begun to view Abel's death as some sort of atoning sacrifice:

"And it came to pass, that Abram fell on his face, and called upon the name of the Lord.

"And God talked with him, saying, My people have gone astray from my precepts, and have not kept mine ordinances, which I gave unto their fathers;

"And they have not observed mine anointing, and the burial, or baptism wherewith I commanded them;

"But have turned from the commandment, and taken unto

themselves the washing of children, and the blood of sprinkling;

"And have said that the blood of the righteous Abel was shed for sins; and have not known wherein they are accountable before me" (JST Genesis 17:3–7).

In other words, due to apostasy in patriarchal times, Abel's proper identity as a type, shadow, and similitude of the future Redeemer became confused and perverted so that Abel eventually came to be regarded as the redeemer of the people in the place of the promised Messiah who was to come to earth in the meridian of time to shed his blood for the sins and sicknesses of the human family (Alma 7:11–14). A profound similitude of the Savior began to be looked upon as though he were the real Savior. Perhaps that is why explicit attention is drawn, in the writings of the antediluvian patriarchs, to the true Messiah who "should come in the meridian of time" (Moses 5:57) and not any other time. Abel's mistaken identity is a remarkable witness to the power of similitudes to teach as well as to mislead when viewed without the Lord's Spirit to provide faithful interpretation.

The parallel between Abel and Christ may be taken even further. While Adam's son Abel was a similitude of Christ, Adam's other son Cain became a significant representation of Satan. In fact, Cain was ultimately placed in the position of ruling over Satan (Moses 5:23, 31). Cain was wicked, just as Satan was wicked. Cain chose Satan over the Lord and was irretrievably overpowered by the adversary. Cain was cast out of his father's presence for wickedness just as Satan was cast out of his Father's presence for wickedness. On the other hand, the brother of Cain, Abel, and the brother of Satan, Christ, were both righteous and carried out the will of their fathers. Put in these terms we see even more clearly the close parallel between two sets of brothers: Abel versus Cain, and Jesus versus Satan (Lucifer). The mortal set, Abel and Cain, point us to the immortal set, Jesus and Lucifer/Satan, as the accompanying chart illustrates.

Cain	opposed	Abel	mortal brothers
Lucifer	opposed	Christ	immortal brothers
Evil		Righteous	
Joined in conspiracy		Were murdered (premeditated)	
Were cast out of their father's presence		Did their father's will	

ENOCH

Enoch was the sixth-great-grandson of father Adam. To read everything about him in the King James Version of the Bible takes less than a minute. But thanks again to the restored information found in Joseph Smith's translation of Genesis (the book of Moses), we now know Enoch as a mighty prophet, seer, and revelator and profound similitude of Christ. In fact, his life and ministry centered mightily on Jesus Christ.

As do all true prophets, Enoch possessed the testimony of Jesus (Revelation 19:10). Armed with this knowledge, he led the people of the city of Zion. Like the future Messiah, Enoch was a savior to his people, working great righteousness and preaching the gospel of Jesus Christ. So successful was he, and so receptive

were his subjects, that together they established Zion, were translated, and taken to heaven. The Lord even said to Enoch that the
city would be his abode forever. Enoch ended up dwelling with
Christ, living in the same eternal community, where the law of
the celestial kingdom governs everything (D&C 105:3–5). Here
is Moses' account of Enoch's accomplishment:

"And the Lord called his people Zion, because they were of
one heart and one mind, and dwelt in righteousness; and there
was no poor among them.

"And Enoch continued his preaching in righteousness unto
the people of God. And it came to pass in his days, that he built
a city that was called the City of Holiness, even Zion.

"And it came to pass that Enoch talked with the Lord; and
he said unto the Lord: Surely Zion shall dwell in safety forever.
But the Lord said unto Enoch: Zion have I blessed, but the
residue of the people have I cursed.

"And it came to pass that the Lord showed unto Enoch all
the inhabitants of the earth; and he beheld, and lo, Zion, in
process of time, was taken up into heaven. And the Lord said
unto Enoch: Behold mine abode forever" (Moses 7:18–21).

As a seer, Enoch "beheld also things which were not visible
to the natural eye, and from thenceforth came the saying abroad
in the land: A seer hath the Lord raised up" (Moses 6:36). This
certainly foreshadowed and imitated the work of the Great
Seer—Jesus Christ. (We note, for example, the seeric powers of
Jesus in his calling of Nathanael; John 1:47–51.) Some of the
most stunning things Enoch saw pertained to the first and second comings of Jesus Christ (see, for example, Moses 7:47–65).
He witnessed in vision "the Son of Man lifted up on the cross,
after the manner of men" (Moses 7:55) and saw the creations of
God mourn and the earth groan at the death of their God

(Moses 7:56). In similitude of Jesus Christ, Enoch himself knew personally of the persecution experienced by the Savior, for "all men were offended because of him" (Moses 6:37). This was precisely Jesus' experience (Matthew 11:6; 26:31) as well as the experience of those who followed him (Matthew 24:10).

Finally, Enoch experienced the same unity with God that the Father and the Son enjoy. The Lord said to his seer: "Behold my Spirit is upon you, . . . *and thou shalt abide in me, and I in you;* therefore walk with me" (Moses 6:34; emphasis added). This promise not only prefigured the words Jesus prayed on the eve of Gethsemane during his great high priestly, or intercessory, prayer (John 17:21) but also parallels Jesus' expressions during his teaching sessions and prayers with the Nephites after his resurrection (3 Nephi 11:27; 19:23, 29). Enoch was an impressive witness, similitude, and foreshadowing of Jesus Christ.

NOAH

There were ten generations from Adam through Noah, each led by a righteous patriarch: Adam, Seth, Enos, Cainan, Mahalaleel, Jared, Enoch, Methuselah, Lamech, and Noah. Each of these patriarchs pointed to Jesus Christ in different ways, but, like Enoch, Noah is particularly noteworthy in this regard.

The name Noah, given by his father, literally means "rest" or "comfort" and immediately points us to him who is the ultimate giver of comfort and rest—Jesus of Nazareth. He bids *all* who labor and are heavy laden to come to him to find ultimate rest (Matthew 11:28–29). When only ten years old, Noah was ordained to the priesthood, an unusually young age for the patriarchs to possess "the Holy Priesthood, after the Order of the Son of God" (D&C 107:3). This order was a type and shadow of the Messiah who was to come.

Like Jesus, Noah was a preacher of righteousness who declared the doctrine of Christ—faith, repentance, baptism, and the gift of the Holy Ghost (compare Moses 8:23–24 and 3 Nephi 11:30–40). Like Jesus, Noah was threatened with death at the hands of enemies and unbelievers. And like Jesus, Noah was preserved in dangerous moments to allow him to pursue his divinely appointed mission (compare Moses 8:18, 26 and Luke 4:29–30), though ultimately Jesus surrendered his life.

Jesus was sinless and perfect (2 Corinthians 5:21; 1 Peter 2:22; Hebrews 4:15). He walked and talked with God, his Father (JST Matthew 4:1; John 11:41). As a similitude and foreshadowing of Jesus, Noah was called "perfect in his generation; and he walked with God" (Moses 8:27). Though Jesus is the true Lord of heaven and earth (Psalm 24:1), Noah, in the likeness of the Lord, received dominion over the earth and all living things in his time.[2] Noah, like Adam, "was the father of all living in this day" and the giver of life in the likeness of Jesus the Messiah.[3] Noah fulfilled the prophecy of his grandfather Methuselah "that from his loins should spring all the kingdoms of the earth (through Noah)" (Moses 8:3).

Finally, Noah returned to earth as the angel Gabriel, after his mortal mission was completed, to announce the births of both John the Baptist and Jesus Christ.[4] Eighteen centuries later, Noah—again as Gabriel—visited the Prophet Joseph Smith to restore priesthood keys (D&C 128:21), which constitute the authority to oversee and direct God's power. Noah will return to earth after Christ's second coming to attend the marriage supper of the Lamb (D&C 27:5–7). Not only was Noah a minister of the Lord but his life and actions demonstrate that he was a similitude and a foreshadowing of Jesus Christ.

CHAPTER 4

MELCHIZEDEK
KING OF RIGHTEOUSNESS

Melchizedek was a great high priest, prophet, and leader who lived after the Flood and during the time of father Abraham. The very name-title of this patriarch points us to Jesus Christ. In the Hebrew language, *melchi-zedek* means "King of Righteousness." Besides referring to the ancient king of the city of Salem, it applies to the Lord Jesus Christ. In addition, the scriptures of the Restoration tell us that Melchizedek was also known as the Prince of Peace (Alma 13:18; JST Genesis 14:33); King of Heaven (JST Genesis 14:36); and King of Peace (JST Genesis 14:36; Hebrews 7:2). All of these titles also denote the roles and mission of Jesus Christ. There is no Old Testament personage whose titles and designations point more clearly to the Savior than do those of Melchizedek.

Melchizedek "exercised mighty faith, and received the office of the high priesthood according to the holy order of God" (Alma 13:18). The Prophet taught that Melchizedek held "the key and the power of endless life" and explained how that power applies to all of the faithful in the latter days:

"What was the power of Melchizedek? 'Twas not the Priesthood of Aaron which administers in outward ordinances, and the offering of sacrifices. Those holding the fulness of the Melchizedek Priesthood are kings and priests of the Most High God, holding the keys of power and blessings. In fact, that Priesthood is a perfect law of theocracy, and stands as God to give laws to the people, administering endless lives to the sons and daughters of Adam."[1]

In truth, Melchizedek himself stood in the place of the Lord and was regarded as being like the Son of God, as evidenced by the renaming of the high priesthood in his honor. As the Lord revealed:

"There are, in the church, two priesthoods, namely, the Melchizedek and Aaronic, including the Levitical Priesthood.

"Why the first is called the Melchizedek Priesthood is because Melchizedek was such a great high priest.

"Before his day it was called *the Holy Priesthood, after the Order of the Son of God.*

"But out of respect or reverence to the name of the Supreme Being, to avoid the too frequent repetition of his name, they, the church, in ancient days, called the priesthood after Melchizedek, or the Melchizedek Priesthood" (D&C 107:1–4).

Furthermore, "the priesthood held by Melchizedek is the very priesthood promised the Son of God during his mortal sojourn, which is to say that Christ was to be like unto Melchizedek."[2] This insight helps to explain Paul's comment in Hebrews 7:15 that the Messiah came "after the similitude of Melchisedec," who prefigured the person of Jesus Christ. Melchizedek was an impressive type and foreshadowing of him who was to come.

Possessing both the kingship of Salem (which Josephus and many other ancient and modern authorities have identified as

Jerusalem) and the keys of the high priesthood, Melchizedek was able to effect mighty changes among his people.[3] Thus, he modeled the roles fulfilled by Jesus Christ as prophet, priest, and king. Melchizedek preached repentance to a group who had waxed strong in iniquity and abomination, who had *all* gone astray, and who were full of all manner of wickedness (Alma 13:17). The people did repent, and Melchizedek established peace in the land (Alma 13:18). Like the Savior, Melchizedek was an instrument in God's hands to redeem his people from spiritual death and destruction.

Melchizedek presided over priesthood power and administered priesthood ordinances to accomplish the Lord's work (Alma 13:15). Even the priesthood was a type of Christ, "given . . . that the people might look forward on the Son of God, it [priesthood power] being a type of his order, or it being his order, and this that they might look forward to him for a remission of their sins, that they might enter into the rest of the Lord" (Alma 13:16). Elder McConkie taught that the ordinances themselves were a type and a foreshadowing of Jesus Christ:

"Every shout of praise and exultation to the Lord Jehovah was Messianic in nature, for those who so acclaimed worshiped the Father in the name of Jehovah-Messiah who would come to redeem his people.

"And so with every baptism, every priesthood ordination, every patriarchal blessing, every act of administering to the sick, every divine ordinance or performance ordained of God, every sacrifice, symbolism, and similitude; all that God ever gave to his people—all was ordained and established in such a way as to testify of his Son and center the faith of believing people in him and in the redemption he was foreordained to make."[4]

The term "rest of the Lord" used by Alma when discussing

Melchizedek (Alma 13:16) is defined by the Lord as "the fulness of his glory" (D&C 84:24). So completely successful was Melchizedek in administering the power and ordinances of the priesthood, and so faithful were his people in living by them, that they actually did enter into the Lord's rest and did enjoy the glory of the Lord—they "did establish peace in the land in his days" (Alma 13:18). In other words, they were translated. Melchizedek and his people became exactly like Enoch and his people.

From another revelation given to Joseph Smith we learn:

"Now Melchizedek was a man of faith, who wrought righteousness; and when a child he feared God, and stopped the mouths of lions, and quenched the violence of fire.

"And thus, having been approved of God, he was ordained an high priest after the order of the covenant which God made with Enoch. . . .

"And men having this faith, coming up unto this order of God, were translated and taken up into heaven.

"And now, Melchizedek was a priest of this order; therefore he obtained peace in Salem, and was called the Prince of peace.

"And his people wrought righteousness, and obtained heaven, and sought for the city of Enoch which God had before taken, separating it from the earth, having reserved it unto the latter days, or the end of the world;

"And hath said, and sworn with an oath, that the heavens and the earth should come together; and the sons of God should be tried so as by fire.

"And this Melchizedek, having thus established righteousness, was called the king of heaven by his people, or, in other words, the King of peace" (JST Genesis 14:26–36).

Melchizedek and his people were taken into heaven, just as

the city of Enoch had been and just as Jesus Christ would be. Obedience to the ordinances of the priesthood was a crucial factor. What ordinances did Melchizedek administer and institute? Certainly baptism, the gift of the Holy Ghost, and ordination—which are easy to understand as types and similitudes of the life of Christ. For example, regarding baptism, the apostle Paul taught: "Therefore we are buried with him by baptism into death: that like as Christ was raised up from the dead by the glory of the Father, even so we also should walk in newness of life. For if we have been planted together in the likeness of his death, we shall be also in the likeness of his resurrection: Knowing this, that our old man is crucified with him, that the body of sin might be destroyed, that henceforth we should not serve sin" (Romans 6:4–6).

Various sources also indicate that the ordinances Melchizedek practiced included the most sacred of all ordinances, which modern disciples of the Savior can find only in houses of the Lord or temples. The Prophet Joseph Smith taught:

"It was the design of the councils of heaven before the world was, that the principles and laws of the priesthood should be predicated upon the gathering of the people in every age of the world. . . . Ordinances instituted in the heavens before the foundation of the world, in the priesthood, for the salvation of men, are not to be altered or changed. All must be saved on the same principles.

"It is for the same purpose that God gathers together His people in the last days, to build unto the Lord a house to prepare them for the ordinances and endowments, washings and anointings, etc. . . .

"If a man gets a fullness of the priesthood of God he has to get it in the same way that Jesus Christ obtained it, and that was by keeping all the commandments and obeying all the ordinances of the house of the Lord."[5]

Facsimile 2 in the book of Abraham largely expresses temple symbolism. The explanation of figure 3 states: "Is made to represent God, sitting upon his throne, clothed with power and authority; with a crown of eternal light upon his head; representing also the grand Key-words of the Holy Priesthood, as revealed to Adam in the Garden of Eden, as also to Seth, Noah, Melchizedek, Abraham, and all to whom the Priesthood was revealed" (Abraham, Facsimile 2). As further noted, these things can only be had and discussed in our day in the "Holy Temple of God" (Abraham, Facsimile 2, figure 8).

A further clue to Melchizedek's temple-oriented ministry is found in the works of Josephus. Writing about the history of Jerusalem after its capture and destruction by the Romans, he preserved this tradition:

"And thus was Jerusalem taken, in the second year of the reign of Vespasian. . . . It had been taken five times before, though this was the second time of its desolation. . . . But he who first built it was a potent man among the Canaanites, and is in our tongue called [Melchisedek] the Righteous King, for such he really was; on which account he was [there] the first priest of God, and first built a temple, [there] and called the city Jerusalem, which was formerly called Salem. However, David, the king of the Jews, ejected the Canaanites, and settled his own people therein."[6]

Though we have no other record of a temple existing in Jerusalem during Melchizedek's day, it seems foolish to dismiss the possibility. It fits well with what we do know about the history and destiny of Melchizedek and his people. Melchizedek held the power of endless lives, the fulness of the priesthood.

He had to get it the same way all others did—through the ordinances of the house of the Lord, which are centered in Jesus Christ and his atonement. Melchizedek taught the ordinances of salvation and was able to change the course of his people from all manner of wickedness and abomination to total righteousness. He and his people sought for the glory of heaven and were translated, joining Enoch's city (JST Genesis 14:32–34). They will return with Jesus Christ at the Second Coming, in like manner as the disciples in New Testament times saw Jesus go into heaven (Acts 1:11; Ether 13:3–6).

Melchizedek was an impressive type and foreshadowing of Jesus Christ in another way: with regard to the administration of the sacrament. We have been taught by Elder Bruce R. McConkie that the sacrament of the Lord's Supper "had its beginning as an authorized ordinance and as a required rite when Jesus and his apostolic witnesses celebrated the feast of the Passover during the week of our Lord's passion."[7] I believe that this is true doctrine. I am equally convinced, based on Joseph Smith's translation of Genesis 14:17–18, that the official institution of the sacrament as a required ritual was "prefigured, some two thousand years before its formal institution among men, when 'Melchizedek, king of Salem, brought forth bread and wine; . . . he being the priest of the most high God. And he gave to Abram' (JST, Gen. 14:17–18). It will be administered after the Lord comes again, to all the faithful of all ages, as they in resurrected glory assemble before him."[8]

Finally, Melchizedek was not only a type and shadow, a prefiguring, of the meridian Messiah, but also one of the best examples in scripture of a foreshadowing of the coming of the millennial Messiah. Alma emphasized that Melchizedek established peace in the land and reigned under his father in Salem

(Alma 13:18). In like fashion, when Christ comes again to the earth, he will establish peace in the land, be called the Prince of Peace, rule as King of the Earth, rule from Salem (Old Jerusalem) as well as New Jerusalem, and rule under the direction of his Father. Truly, Melchizedek's life prefigured Christ's.

CHAPTER 5

ABRAHAM, ISAAC, AND JACOB

FATHERS OF THE FAITHFUL

Perhaps the most easily recognizable type, shadow, and similitude of Jesus of Nazareth in the Old Testament is the patriarch Isaac. His supreme faithfulness and obedience in the face of life-threatening circumstances stands as a towering example of Christlike submissiveness. Abraham's willingness to offer his son Isaac and Isaac's willingness to follow his father's will that he be offered as a sacrifice are powerfully and poignantly summarized for us by the prophet Jacob:

"For, for this intent have we written these things, that they may know that we knew of Christ, and we had a hope of his glory many hundred years before his coming; and not only we ourselves had a hope of his glory, but also all the holy prophets which were before us.

"Behold, they believed in Christ and worshiped the Father in his name, and also we worship the Father in his name. And for this intent we keep the law of Moses, it pointing our souls to him, and for this cause it is sanctified unto us for righteousness, even as it was accounted unto Abraham in the wilderness to be obedient unto the commands of God in offering up his son Isaac, which is a similitude of God and his Only Begotten Son" (Jacob 4:4–5).

This similitude, then, is even more profound than the rest of the religious world has supposed. Isaac's actions parallel Christ's; Abraham's actions parallel those of God the Father. The whole episode presents similitudes and parallels of staggering proportions when we think about it. It is a story of sacrifice for all humankind. Remember, the word *sacrifice* derives from a combination of two Latin words—*sacer,* "sacred," and *facere,* "to make"—so to sacrifice is "to make sacred." Just as the sacrifice of God's Son—that incomprehensible act by which all things are "made sacred" or brought into reconciliation from a state of estrangement—is for all mankind, so too the lessons of Abraham's sacrifice are for all to learn. Abraham's sacrifice instructs us more perfectly about God and his Son. Knowledge of mortal sacrifice brings us to an understanding of godly sacrifice.

Here we remember the impressive discourse of Elder Melvin J. Ballard who said that he thought, as he read the story of Abraham's sacrifice of his son Isaac, that our Father was trying "to tell us what it cost him to give his Son as a gift to the world. . . . It must have pierced the heart of Father Abraham to hear the trusting and confiding son say: 'You have forgotten the sacrifice.' Looking at the youth, his son of promise, the poor father could only say: 'The Lord will provide.'

"They ascended the mountain, gathered the stones together, and placed the fagots upon them. Then Isaac was bound, hand and foot, kneeling upon the altar. I presume Abraham, like a true father, must have given his son his farewell kiss, his blessing, his love, and his soul must have been drawn out in that hour of agony toward this son who was to die by the hand of his own father. Every step proceeded until the cold steel was drawn, and the hand raised that was to strike the blow to let out the life's blood. Then the angel of the Lord said: 'It is enough.'

"Our Father in heaven went through all that and more, for in his case the hand was not stayed. He loved his Son Jesus Christ, better than Abraham ever loved Isaac, . . . yet he allowed this well-beloved Son to descend from his place of glory and honor, where millions did him homage, down to the earth, a condescension that is not within the power of man to conceive of."[1]

The story of Abraham's offering up his son, the son of the birthright as well as of the covenant (Genesis 17:15–19), is well documented in Genesis 22. God had repeatedly promised Abraham an innumerable posterity as one of the terms of the covenant established between Deity and the great patriarch (Genesis 12:2; 15:1–6; 17:2–6, 15–19). The promise came as a result of the nature of the covenant (to offer exaltation to all; Abraham 2:6–11 and D&C 132:29–50) and as a response to Abraham's unyielding desire "to be a father of many nations" (Abraham 1:2). After long years of waiting, Isaac was born, a tangible beginning to God's promise of a posterity as numerous as the stars in heaven (Genesis 15:5). But a few years after Isaac was born, God called upon Abraham again and in an instant turned his world upside down. "And it came to pass after these things, that God did tempt Abraham, and said unto him, Abraham: and he said, Behold, here I am. And he said, Take now thy son, thine only son Isaac, whom thou lovest, and get thee into the land of Moriah; and offer him there for a burnt offering upon one of the mountains which I will tell thee of" (Genesis 22:1–2).

The Hebrew word *nissah,* translated as "tempt" in the King James Version, should be translated as "test," according to every Hebrew dictionary I know of. God tested Abraham, on purpose! The structure of this portion of the narrative, especially in Hebrew, denotes an immediate reply on the part of the patriarch. This is an important lesson for us. Do we respond quickly to a call from the Lord, or even to the impressions of the Spirit? Abraham did.

The rest of the story in Genesis 22, called the *Akedah* (Hebrew, "binding of Isaac"), is told succinctly. But the economy of language only serves to emphasize and make more poignant the many successive similitudes, types, and foreshadowings of Jesus Christ. Rather than focus on the story, let us consider some of the powerful parallels between Abraham and Isaac, and our Eternal Father and Jesus Christ:

1. *Name-titles.* Just as Jesus Christ was God's Only Begotten Son, whom the Father gave as the great and last sacrifice (John 3:16), so Isaac is referred to by God as Abraham's "only son," whom Abraham gave as a sacrifice (Genesis 22:2, 16). In fact, the apostle Paul makes this connection more explicitly: "By faith Abraham, when he was tried, offered up Isaac: and he that had received the promises offered up his *only begotten son*" (Hebrews 11:17; emphasis added). Only two figures in our English-language scriptures are referred to by the designation "only begotten son." One is Jesus Christ, and the other is Isaac.

2. *Timing.* Just as Jesus was up early in the morning on the last day of his mortal life to face the events that led to the fulfillment of his sacrifice (Mark 14:68–15:1), so Abraham and Isaac "rose up early in the morning" to travel to fulfill their eventual sacrifice (Genesis 22:3). The reference to their arrival at the place of sacrifice "on the third day" is very likely more

than just coincidence, because the Atonement was completed "on the third day" when Jesus rose from the dead as prophesied (Mosiah 3:10; D&C 20:23).

In addition to the parallel with Jesus' life, there is an interesting lesson to be gleaned from Abraham's response in rising early in the morning to do God's will. In this context, President Spencer W. Kimball asked, "How often do Church members arise early in the morning to do the will of the Lord? How often do we say, 'Yes, I will have home evening with my family, but the children are so young now; I will start when they are older?' How often do we say, 'Yes, I will obey the commandment to store food and to help others, but just now I have neither the time nor the money to spare; I will obey later?'"[2]

Abraham did not dally to obey, though he very well could have done so in the hope that God would change his mind in the meantime. Elder Theodore M. Burton observed, "Neither did he dare delay action lest his heart fail and cause him to falter in his determination to obey the Lord."[3]

3. *Travel.* Just as Jesus traveled to the place of his eventual sacrifice on a donkey to make his triumphal entry into Jerusalem (Matthew 21:1–7), so Isaac rode on a donkey to the place of his eventual sacrifice (Genesis 22:3).

4. *Wood.* Just as Jesus carried the wooden cross to the site of his crucifixion (John 19:16–17), so Isaac carried the wood for his sacrifice to the place of the altar (Genesis 22:6). On Moriah, Abraham built an altar. The Hebrew word for altar, *mizbeah,* is derived from the word for sacrifice, *zebah.* Thus, "altar" literally means "the place of sacrificing." But where did Abraham's sacrifice of Isaac occur?

In rabbinic and Talmudic times, the phrase "building an altar" was used as a metaphor to mean not only the observance of the commandments but also the total consecration of all one possessed—even the laying down of one's life—for the sanctification of God's name. Some of the ancient rabbinic sages, therefore, coined expressions like "as if an altar was erected in his heart" to portray those individuals who were willing to do all that God required. Some of them well understood that sacrifice was first made in the mind and heart of the offerer. Their exemplar was Abraham. He had erected an altar in his heart long before he reached Moriah.

Things are not so different today. We talk about being ready to "lay it all on the altar." We covenant at altars to sacrifice all we possess for the Lord, and in doing so we "build altars in our hearts," as the rabbis said. Our exemplar is also Abraham. On this point the two great branches of latter-day Israel, Joseph and Judah, are as one. Yet latter-day Joseph goes beyond this. For while Abraham is an exemplar, Christ is *the* great exemplar! Said he: "For I came down from heaven, not to do my own will but the will of him that sent me" (John 6:38). Long before any of us were sent to this earth, Christ understood the principle of true and total sacrifice. In premortality he became the foreordained Savior of mankind, a pure sacrifice for sin as a lamb without blemish or spot (1 Peter 1:19–20). In premortality, to use the language of the rabbis, Jesus Christ had "built an altar in his heart."

5. *Lamb.* Just as Jesus was the Lamb chosen by the Father—"slain from the foundation of the world" (Moses 7:47; Revelation 13:8)—so Isaac was the lamb chosen by God to fulfill the sacrifice (Genesis 22:7–8).

6. *Loyalty.* Just as God did not withhold his Only Begotten Son from the world (John 3:16) and kept his promise made in the beginning (Abraham 3:27), so Abraham was recognized by

God for keeping his promises: "For now I know that thou fearest God, seeing thou hast not withheld thy son, thine only son from me" (Genesis 22:12).

7. *Location.* Just as Jesus appeared many times on Mount Moriah, which is the Jerusalem temple site (2 Chronicles 3:1), so Isaac's sacrifice on Mount Moriah foreshadowed the appearances of Jesus and prefigured in particular the crucifixion of Jesus Christ. In this connection, it is significant that after Isaac had been rescued and the ram in the thicket had been offered as a sacrifice in Isaac's place, Abraham called the name of the spot where all these things had occurred "Jehovah-jireh: as it is said to this day, In the mount of the Lord it shall be seen" (Genesis 22:14). A literal rendering of the Hebrew term *Jehovah-jireh* is "Jehovah will see" or "Jehovah will be seen." And a perfectly acceptable alternate translation of Genesis 22:14 could read: "In this mountain Jehovah will be seen." And so it was—in the meridian of time.

Though we have emphasized Isaac's example as a magnificent, perhaps unequaled, similitude of the Son, and Abraham's actions as a similitude of the Father's, in truth Abraham also points us to Jesus Christ and stands as an impressive similitude of the Savior, fulfilling a dual role. His experience with Isaac undoubtedly helped Abraham to see the Savior's future crucifixion from the Father's perspective. (Perhaps that is why Hebrews 11:17 refers to Isaac as Abraham's "only begotten son," even though Abraham had already fathered Ishmael.) Just as significant, however, for understanding the Atonement was Abraham's own earlier experience with human sacrifice, recorded in Abraham 1, because that horrible episode placed Abraham in a role or position like that of the Son. Few other mortals, if any, would be thus prepared to comprehend the atoning sacrifice from the perspective of both the Father and the Son.

Abraham's apostate father very nearly had him killed on an altar dedicated to the false gods of Chaldea and Egypt. It was only by the intervention of an angel from God that his life was preserved (Abraham 1:5–17). Thus, he "knew from personal experience how horrible human sacrifice could be."[4] And therein lies part of the test, for, when Abraham was an old man, after years of faithful living, God turned the tables on him. Contradiction became an integral and inescapable part of Abraham's experience. Can we fathom the unspeakable anguish with which Abraham contemplated the request to make Isaac the object of this gruesome form of ritual killing—a request made by the very same God who had once saved Abraham from certain death and later condemned human sacrifice? Would this not have been seen by Abraham as the supreme contradiction of his life?

Not only that but Abraham had been promised an innumerable posterity and continuation of the covenant through Isaac. Through this son of the promise, Abraham's hopes for the future were to be realized. Yet, the very same God who had made those covenant promises with Abraham was also requiring Abraham to offer up Isaac as a sacrifice. That sacrifice, once offered, would be complete in its results—nothing left—for, as Abraham knew, a burnt offering was to be wholly consumed. Would not Abraham have been forced to confront the unmitigated nature of this contradiction from its inception?

How like Jesus Christ was Abraham. Jesus faced the supreme contradiction of history and suffered infinitely in Gethsemane and on Golgotha's cross. God, the greatest of all, the very Prince of Peace, suffered the greatest contradiction of all. Abraham was a great and noble follower of righteousness, desiring to be a "prince of peace" (Abraham 1:2), and yet he suffered the effects of great contradiction. The Prophet Joseph Smith taught that Jesus Christ "descended in suffering below that which man can suffer; or, in other words, suffered greater sufferings, and was exposed to more *powerful contradictions* than any man can be. But, notwithstanding all this, he kept the law of God."[5]

This has to be one of the greatest lessons of mortality. All sons and daughters of God, all disciples of the Lord, will suffer contradictions, but all must demonstrate their faithfulness and loyalty in the face of that contradiction. Sacred history shows that all the noble and great among our Father's children have experienced contradiction in their lives.

In Abraham's case, the contradiction is unmistakable. In the lives of others, perhaps even in our own lives, the contradictions may seem less dramatic, though, in truth, they are no less important. The contradictions vary. The just suffer injustice. The peace-loving face violence or war. The loyal are treated disloyally. Sometimes circumstances in life seem to work against us, though we try with extra effort to live righteously. Perhaps it looks, at times, as though God has withdrawn his influence rather than eased our burden at the very moment when we think we need his help and comfort the most. Perhaps our trials increase though our obedience becomes more exact and our performance more exemplary. Sometimes life becomes grossly unfair.

Here we may turn to a modern apostle whose teachings instruct us in a more perfect way. Elder Neal A. Maxwell said:

" 'If it's fair, it is not a true trial!' That is, without the added presence of some inexplicableness and some irony and injustice, the experience may not stretch us or lift us sufficiently. The crucifixion of Christ was clearly the greatest injustice in human history, but the Savior bore up under it with majesty and indescribable valor.

"Paul indicated that 'there was *given* to me a thorn in the flesh.' (2 Corinthians 12:7–9. Italics added.) Use of the word *given* suggests that Paul knew wherefrom this affliction came. Further, as it must be with anyone who seeks sainthood, Paul had to be 'willing to submit to all things which the Lord seeth fit to inflict upon him.' (Mosiah 3:19.)."[6]

Every disciple of the Lord and true follower of Abraham will face the kind of tests, trials, and contradictions the great patriarch faced. These will be different for every person, but they will come! The Lord said that those who profess discipleship "must needs be chastened and tried, even as Abraham, who was commanded to offer up his only son. For all those who will not endure chastening, but deny me, cannot be sanctified" (D&C 101:4–5).

Beside the Savior, Abraham is the standard for mortals to live by. He mirrored the behavior of the Father on the one hand and of the Son on the other. He faced contradiction and maintained his absolute loyalty to Deity and eternal principles. Such tests are given to mortals and are calculated to allow us the opportunity to demonstrate our loyalty just as Abraham demonstrated his. God doesn't want much—he wants everything. And he desires with all his soul to give us back everything he possesses. We are asked to give up all in order to receive an infinitely greater all.

The magnitude of the promise is almost incomprehensible, and the unevenness of the offer staggering: everything we possess in exchange for everything God possesses! Why would any of us be unwilling to sacrifice all we have been given, all that is not even ours to begin with? President George Q. Cannon said:

"There is no sacrifice that God can ask of us or His servants whom He has chosen to lead us that we should hesitate about making. In one sense of the word it is no sacrifice. We may call it so because it comes in contact with our selfishness and our unbelief; but it ought not to come in contact with our faith. . . .

"Why did the Lord ask such things of Abraham? Because, knowing what his future would be and that he would be the father of an innumerable posterity, he was determined to test him. God did not do this for His own sake for He knew by His foreknowledge what Abraham would do; but the purpose was to impress upon Abraham a lesson and to enable him to attain unto knowledge that he could not obtain in any other way. That is why God tries all of us. It is not for His own knowledge, for He knows all things beforehand. He knows all your lives and everything you will do. But he tries us for our own good that we may know ourselves; for it is most important that a man should know himself.

"He required Abraham to submit to this trial because He intended to give him glory, exaltation and honor; He intended to make him a king and a priest, to share with Himself the glory, power and dominion which He exercised."[7]

Abraham did become a king and a priest of the Most High. He became the friend of God and father of the faithful (James 2:23; D&C 138:41). A remarkable legacy was passed on to the children of Abraham by their father. Those children included Jacob, grandson of the great patriarch and heir to the promises of God. Impressively, Jacob also was a similitude of Jesus Christ. Like Jesus he interacted with God and angels (compare

Genesis 28:12–13 and JST Matthew 4:1, 11); he saw God face to face (compare Genesis 32:30 and Matthew 17:1–5); and his name, when changed, reflected God's direct involvement in the affairs of humankind (compare *Israel,* "let God prevail," and *Jesus* or *Yeshua,* "God saves").

As similitudes, types, and foreshadowings of Jesus Christ in so many ways, is it any wonder that the great patriarchs Abraham, Isaac, and Jacob have become exactly like God, "they have entered into their exaltation, according to the promises, and sit upon thrones, and are not angels but are gods" (D&C 132:37). Such is the legacy left to us in modern times. When we commit to accepting the gospel covenant, the Abrahamic covenant, we become the literal, actual seed of Abraham, and the Church and kingdom, and the elect of God (D&C 84:34).[8]

CHAPTER 6

JOSEPH OF EGYPT
THE FIRST OF MANY

The story of Joseph the patriarch is given much attention in Genesis and forms its own unit in the last section of that book of scripture (chapters 37–50). He was the firstborn son of Jacob (Israel) and Rachel, Jacob's second wife (Genesis 30:22–24; 37:3). Among the twelve sons of Jacob, the fathers of the twelve tribes, Joseph was given the birthright because Reuben, the firstborn of Jacob's first wife, Leah, lost that position of family leadership due to immorality (1 Chronicles 5:1–2). His coat of many colors seems "to have been the badge of the birthright which had been forfeited by Reuben and transferred to Joseph."[1] Joseph enjoyed a favored status with his father, Jacob (Genesis 37:3). A precocious young man, Joseph may not have been tactful in discussing his birthright, but he possessed the gift of revelation (Genesis 37:5–10; 39:7–20). His brothers grew jealous of their younger brother and plotted to kill him (Genesis 37:11–25). But Judah persuaded his brothers to sell Joseph to merchants who were on their way to Egypt, and there he was eventually purchased by Potiphar, an officer of Pharaoh and captain of the guard (Genesis 37:26–36).

In Egypt, Joseph achieved great success as well as fame and

showed himself to be one of Israel's greatest prophets, patriarchs, and political leaders. He proved himself a man of sterling character and impeccable morality, especially in the matter involving Potiphar's duplicitous and immoral wife (Genesis 39:5–20). The Lord was continually with Joseph. Even though Joseph was cast into prison for a time, his integrity, ability, and spirituality eventually helped him to rise to the position of "ruler over all the land of Egypt" (Genesis 41:43). He has served as a model of integrity in the face of almost insurmountable injustice for more than thirty centuries.

Perhaps Joseph's greatest legacy was his saving the house of Israel from destruction due to famine (Genesis 41:56–57). This included his father's family as well as his brothers and their families, even though they had betrayed him years earlier. As the savior of Israel, as well as in many other matters, Joseph is a preeminent similitude of Jesus Christ. He prefigured and foreshadowed many aspects of the life and ministry of the Messiah, our Savior. It is enlightening to review some of the most impressive of these:

1. Joseph was a firstborn son and holder of the birthright in a great family (Genesis 30:22–24; 37:3; 43:33). Jesus Christ was *the* Firstborn and held the birthright (D&C 93:21). In ancient times and under the patriarchal order, the birthright carried certain prerogatives, obligations, opportunities, and blessings and was passed from father to firstborn son (Genesis 43:33). With it came an extra portion of the family inheritance and the right to preside. As the possessor of these benefits, the birthright holder was expected to govern the family in justice and equity, to redeem family members in trouble, to recover forfeited property of a kinsman, or to purchase the freedom of a kinsman if he had fallen into slavery. The birthright itself was

a type and similitude of the Firstborn of the Father, Jesus Christ.[2]

2. Joseph was the favored son of his father (Genesis 37:3). Jesus was the well beloved Son of the Father (Matthew 3:17).

3. Joseph was rejected by his brothers, the house of Israel (Genesis 37:4). Likewise, Jesus "came unto his own, and his own received him not" (John 1:11).

4. Joseph was betrayed and sold into the hands of the Ishmaelites and then to the Egyptians as the result of Judah's urging (Genesis 37:25–27). Jesus was betrayed and sold out to the Jews and Romans through the work of another Judah (Greek, *Judas*) (Matthew 27:3).

5. Joseph was sold for twenty pieces of silver—the price of a slave in his day (Genesis 27:28). Jesus was sold for thirty pieces of silver (Matthew 27:3)—the price of a slave in his day as outlined in the law of Moses (Exodus 21:32). Elder James E. Talmage noted: "Under the impulse of diabolic avarice, which, however, was probably but a secondary element in the real cause of his perfidious treachery, [Judas] bargained to sell his Master for money . . . 'and they covenanted with him for thirty pieces of silver' (Matthew 26:15). This amount, approximately seventeen dollars in our money, but of many times greater purchasing power with the Jews in that day than now with us, was the price fixed by the law as that of a slave; it was also the foreseen sum of the blood-money to be paid for the Lord's betrayal."[3]

The Old Testament prophet Zechariah foresaw Judas's perfidy in vision centuries before it occurred. "And I said unto them, If ye think good, give me my price; and if not, forbear. So they weighed for my price thirty pieces of silver. And the Lord said unto me, Cast it unto the potter: a goodly price that

I was prised at of them. And I took the thirty pieces of silver, and cast them to the potter in the house of the Lord" (Zechariah 11:12–13). Exactly as Zechariah had foreseen, Judas tried to return the thirty pieces of silver after experiencing overwhelming remorse. The chief priests refused the money. Judas then threw down the money in the house of the Lord, and the Jewish leaders subsequently purchased the potter's field with it (Matthew 27:3–10).

6. In their attempt to destroy Joseph, his brothers actually set up the conditions that eventually brought about their own temporal salvation. In parallel fashion, Jewish leaders, in their attempts to destroy Jesus, arranged for the sacrifice of Jesus— which led to the Atonement and their own redemption as well as the temporal and spiritual salvation of all of Israel and all humankind. The words of "O Savior, Thou Who Wearest a Crown" come to mind:

> *Tho craven friends betray thee,*
> *They feel thy love's embrace;*
> *The very foes who slay thee*
> *Have access to thy grace.*
> (Hymns, *no. 197*)

The exclamation of Joseph after his reunion with his family teaches an invaluable lesson about the Lord's planning and ability to use seemingly tragic circumstances to work for the ultimate and eternal good of his children. "And Joseph said unto them, Fear not: for am I in the place of God? But as for you, ye thought evil against me; but God meant it unto good, to bring to pass, as it is this day, to save much people alive" (Genesis 50:19–20). This powerful principle serves to highlight the doctrine taught by the Lord through Isaiah: "For my thoughts are not your thoughts, neither are your ways my ways, saith the Lord. For as the heavens are higher than the earth, so are my ways higher than your ways, and my thoughts than your thoughts" (Isaiah 55:8–9). Man's feeble logic pales in comparison to God's perfect knowledge.

7. Joseph was unjustly accused and punished (Genesis 39:14–20), but he did not become bitter or blame God. He was submissive and even offered to help his fellow convicts (Genesis 40:6–8). Likewise, Jesus was unjustly accused and punished (Matthew 26:65–67; 27:19–50) but did not blame God. He was submissive and offered to help his fellow convicts (Luke 23:39–43). Concerning Jesus' submissiveness, Elder Boyd K. Packer reminds us that what happened to Jesus happened not because Pilate or the Jewish leaders had the power to impose it but because he was willing to accept it.[4]

8. Joseph began his mission of preparing for the salvation of his brothers and sisters at age thirty (Genesis 41:46). Jesus officially began his ministry of preparing the salvation of his brothers and sisters at age thirty (Luke 3:23).

9. When Joseph was finally raised to his exalted position in Egypt, all knees bowed to him (Genesis 41:43). All will eventually bow the knee to Jesus (D&C 88:104).

10. Joseph provided bread for Israel and saved them from death, all without price (Genesis 41:43). Jesus, the Bread of Life, did the same for all mortals (John 6:48–57). As Jacob said of the Savior's offer: "Come, my brethren, every one that thirsteth, come ye to the waters; and he that hath no money, come buy and eat; yea, come buy wine and milk without money and without price" (2 Nephi 9:50).

One of the most touching and telling scenes in all of scripture is also one that ultimately points to the compassionate, merciful nature of the Lord who took up a mortal tabernacle in the meridian of time. When Joseph finally revealed himself to his brothers who had come to Egypt seeking temporal salvation, he forgave them for their mean and depraved actions years earlier, he extended his unmerited love to them, and he acknowledged the goodness of God. Joseph mirrored the character and actions of Jesus of Nazareth.

Another significant legacy left to the world by Joseph is his unparalleled prophecies about the destiny of the house of Israel in general and the future of his own descendants, his own tribe, in particular. Joseph was a choice seer who was privileged to see in vision other choice seers. His prophecies are eloquent testimony and incontrovertible evidence of his expansive understanding of the roles of Moses and Aaron, yet to come, and of a latter-day prophet named Joseph, to be raised up from among his own numerous posterity, who would shepherd the whole house of Israel. A remarkable summary of Joseph's prophecies has been restored in our own day through Joseph Smith's inspired revision of Genesis 50. There we learn the following:

> Joseph of old testified that the Lord had visited him, and he saw the future Egyptian bondage of his people (Genesis 50:24). He spoke as the birthright leader of all Israel, not just as the leader of his own tribe.
>
> He saw that the Lord would raise up a deliverer of his people—not the Messiah but a deliverer from Egyptian bondage (Genesis 50:24). The clear implication is that the deliverer would act and appear very much like the Messiah. This deliverer would himself be a similitude of the Messiah.
>
> Joseph harked back to an earlier prophecy embedded in Judah's patriarchal blessing (Genesis 49:10) and confirmed

that the future Messiah would be called Shilo(h) (Genesis 50:24).

Joseph revealed that the name of the future deliverer of Israel from Egyptian bondage would be Moses (Genesis 50:29).

Joseph foresaw that Moses would gather Israel, lead them as a flock, and smite the waters of the Red Sea with his rod (Genesis 50:34).

Joseph prophesied that Moses would be a judge of his people and that he would not speak many words but write the law of God as given to him by the finger of the Lord's own hand (Genesis 50:35).

And finally, Joseph foretold that the Lord would provide Moses with a spokesman, whose name would be Aaron (Genesis 50:35).

Regarding Joseph's prophecies concerning the future, we easily see how detailed his knowledge was:

Joseph saw both the scattering of Israel and the future American sojourn of a specific branch of his descendants (Genesis 50:25).

Joseph saw that the Messiah would be made manifest unto his descendants in the latter days (Genesis 50:25).

Joseph was told by the Lord directly that He would raise up a choice seer from his posterity, that the choice seer would be highly esteemed among his posterity, and that this choice seer would do a work on behalf of his posterity (Genesis 50:27).

The choice seer would bring Joseph's posterity to a knowledge of covenants made previously with their fathers (Genesis 50:28).

Joseph said he was told by the Lord that this choice seer would be like unto Moses, of whom he had also been prophesying (Genesis 50:29).

Joseph foretold of the complementary nature of the Bible and the Book of Mormon and their great power together in confounding false doctrine. This is the basic message of Ezekiel's testimony as well (Ezekiel 37:15–19), received by Joseph many centuries earlier.

Joseph related how the Lord declared that the choice seer would not simply bring forth God's word but that he would have power to convince Joseph's posterity of the truth of God's word (Genesis 50:30).

Joseph reported that the Lord said He would bless the choice seer and confound those that sought to destroy him, that the choice seer would be named Joseph, and that his father's name would be Joseph (Genesis 50:33).

Great are the prophecies of Joseph of old, and great was the life of this powerful patriarch. He was shaped by the hand of heaven. He, like his future namesake, was visited by the Lord, and he received direct and mighty revelation. He was promised by the Lord that his seed would be preserved forever. In fact, he was also promised that the Lord would *remember* him from "generation to generation" (JST Genesis 50:33). Such language is unique. One remarkable way, among many, that this promise was kept is recorded in the Book of Mormon. When Moroni raised the title of liberty, he declared to his people: "Behold, we are a remnant of the seed of Jacob; yea, we are a remnant of the seed of Joseph, whose coat was rent by his brethren into many pieces; yea, and now behold, let us remember to keep the commandments of God, or our garments shall be rent by our brethren, and we be cast into prison, or be sold, or be slain. Yea, let us preserve our liberty as a remnant of Joseph" (Alma 46:23–24).

Joseph of old was not only a type, a foreshadowing, and a similitude of Jesus Christ and his mission but he was also a similitude of a latter-day Joseph—the man we know as the Prophet Joseph Smith. Among Joseph's last acts as prophet, patriarch, and leader of the house of Israel was his teaching about future dispensations. He tried to prepare Israel to receive Moses and to recognize the great gatherer/deliverer as both Jehovah's anointed and as a type and similitude of the coming Messiah.

CHAPTER 7

MOSES AND JOSHUA
LAWGIVERS AND DELIVERERS

No prophet knew more about the coming of the Messiah, no prophet knew more about messianic types and shadows, and few prophets wrote more about the promised Messiah than Moses—the great lawgiver and deliverer of Israel. These latter roles were themselves profound similitudes and types of Christ. In fact, Moses was told directly by the Lord that he was a similitude of Jesus Christ. After his initial call, when Moses was upon the unnamed mountain, experiencing the encounter recorded in Moses 1, God said to him: "And I have a work for thee, Moses, my son; and thou art in the similitude of mine Only Begotten; and mine Only Begotten is and shall be the Savior, for he is full of grace and truth" (Moses 1:6).

Such explicit and pointed language is truly arresting. Elder Bruce R. McConkie explored the implication of this declaration:

"Moses was in the similitude of Christ, and Christ was like unto Moses. Of all the hosts of our Father's children, these two are singled out as being like each other. All men are created in the image of God, both spiritually and temporally. . . . And all men are endowed with the characteristics and attributes which, in their eternal fulness, dwell in Deity. But it appears there is a special image, a special similitude, a special likeness where the man Moses and the man Jesus are concerned. . . . That is to say, Moses bore the resemblance of his Lord. In appearance, guise, and semblance, they were the same. The qualities of the one were the qualities of the other."[1]

From the very beginning of Moses' life we see specific episodes that foreshadowed episodes from the life of the future earthly Messiah, Jesus of Nazareth. Both were born in perilous times. Both survived kings who attempted to kill male babies around the time of their birth (Exodus 1:15–16; Matthew 2:16–18), and both were saved by their families who were helped by God (Exodus 1:20–2:8; Matthew 2:12–15).

Both Moses and Jesus Christ spent time in Egypt, and both came forth out of Egypt, led by God (Exodus 13:18; Matthew 2:15, 19–21). Both Moses and Jesus were tempted by Satan and had to engage in spiritual combat, so to speak, with the actual personage of Satan (Moses 1:12–22; Matthew 4:3–10).

In studying Moses' experience with Satan, it becomes clear that the great prophet-deliverer was conscious that he was a living similitude of Jesus Christ. It is exciting to see how this knowledge became not only a spiritual anchor to Moses but also a tool of discernment that he used when confronted by the adversary and his temptations. For example, when Satan appeared to Moses immediately after Moses had been transfigured and talked with God face to face (at which time God told him that he was a similitude of his Son), the devil tried to deceive the prophet. Moses used his newly acquired knowledge as a source of strength and discernment to rebuke Satan, and he used some of the same words that Jesus would use some fourteen hundred years later: "And it came to pass that Moses looked upon Satan and said: Who art thou? For behold, I am a son of God, in the similitude of his Only Begotten; and where is thy glory, that I should worship thee? . . . *Get thee hence, Satan;* deceive me not; for God said unto me: Thou art after the similitude of mine Only Begotten" (Moses 1:13–16; emphasis added; compare Matthew 4:10).

Knowing for himself the nature of God and his Only Begotten Son, Moses could tell the difference between God and Satan, between truth and error, between light and darkness, between transfigured glory and the natural man. From this point on, knowing that he was in the similitude of the Son of God, Moses became a mighty prophet of the Messiah. The spirit of prophecy is "the testimony of Jesus" (Revelation 19:10), and Moses possessed this spirit, and thus the power of his prophetic mantle, to the very end. During his final days with Israel, Moses gave the last three speeches of his mortal life. Collectively, these speeches are known as the book of Deuteronomy and were delivered on or near Mount Nebo as the twelve tribes stood poised, ready to cross over into the promised land. In this setting, Moses declared: "The Lord thy God will raise up unto thee a Prophet from the midst of thee, of thy brethren, like unto me; unto him he shall hearken. . . . And the Lord said unto me, . . . I will raise them up a Prophet from among their brethren, like unto thee, and will put my words in his mouth; and he shall speak unto them all that I shall command him. And it shall come to pass, that whosoever will not hearken unto my words which he shall speak in my name, I will require it of him" (Deuteronomy 18:15–19).

Few scriptures in the standard works are as important as this one, at least judged on the basis of where this passage is subsequently quoted and who uses it. It is quoted by Nephi

(1 Nephi 22:21), Peter (Acts 3:22–23), Stephen (Acts 7:37), and Moroni (Joseph Smith–History 1:40), always as a special testimony that Jesus is the literal fulfillment of Moses' words. As the ultimate validation of Moses' declaration, the resurrected Lord himself quoted them: "Behold, I am he of whom Moses spake, saying: A prophet shall the Lord your God raise up unto you of your brethren, like unto me; him shall ye hear in all things whatsoever he shall say unto you. And it shall come to pass that every soul who will not hear that prophet shall be cut off from among the people. Verily I say unto you, yea, and all the prophets from Samuel and those that follow after, as many as have spoken, have testified of me" (3 Nephi 20:23–24).

During his leadership of the tribes of Israel as they sojourned in the wilderness, Moses used one of the most profound and enduring symbols of the Messiah's atonement in all of the Old Testament: "And Moses made a serpent of brass, and put it upon a pole, and it came to pass, that if a serpent had bitten any man, when he beheld the serpent of brass, he lived" (Numbers 21:9).

The brass serpent was a type and a symbol of the redemption of Christ, which he, in part, worked out on the cross. Many prophets testified of this symbol (1 Nephi 17:41; 2 Nephi 25:20; Alma 33:18–22; Helaman 8:13–15), but none more directly or powerfully than Jesus Christ himself. "And as Moses lifted up the serpent in the wilderness, even so must the Son of man be lifted up: That whosoever believeth in him should not perish, but have eternal life" (John 3:14–15).

In using the image of the serpent, Moses was employing a divinely instituted and long-recognized representation of Israel's God. The serpent as a messianic symbol goes back to the

Creation. When Satan came to Eve in the guise of the Messiah—promising things that only the true Messiah could rightly promise ("ye shall not surely die: . . . [but] shall be as gods"; Genesis 3:5)—he used the symbol of the serpent to try to deceive Eve by passing off this messianic symbol as his own (Moses 4:6–10). Later, when Moses stood before Pharaoh and his court, he employed the image and symbol of the serpent to demonstrate the power of Jehovah, whom he represented. The rod Moses threw down became a serpent and swallowed up the serpents of Pharaoh's sorcerers (Exodus 7:10–12). Moses did not do this of himself but upon the previously given instructions of Jehovah, the guarantor of the power behind the symbol of the serpent:

"And Moses answered and said, But, behold, they will not believe me, nor hearken unto my voice: for they will say, The Lord hath not appeared unto thee.

"And the Lord said unto him, What is that in thine hand? And he said, A rod.

"And he said, Cast it on the ground. And he cast it on the ground, and it became a serpent; and Moses fled from before it.

"And the Lord said unto Moses, Put forth thine hand, and take it by the tail. And he put forth his hand, and caught it, and it became a rod in his hand:

"That they may believe that the Lord God of their fathers, the God of Abraham, the God of Isaac, and the God of Jacob, hath appeared unto thee" (Exodus 4:1–5).

Truly, the serpent was an ancient and mighty messianic image.[2]

Other parallels, similitudes, and foreshadowings of Jesus Christ in the life of Moses are plentiful:

Like Jesus Christ, Moses was foreordained to perform

prophetic, salvational, redemptive ministries in behalf of our Heavenly Father's children (JST Genesis 50:24–29; 1 Peter 1:18–20).

Like Jesus Christ, Moses viewed the lands and kingdoms of the earth (Moses 1:27–29; JST Matthew 4:8).

Like Jesus Christ, Moses was meek "above all the men which were upon the face of the earth" (Numbers 12:3; compare Matthew 11:29 and 1 Peter 2:22–23; 3:9).

Like Jesus Christ, Moses controlled the waters and elements (Exodus 14:21–22, 26–27; Matthew 8:26; 14:26; Mark 4:38–39).

Just as Moses provided manna from heaven (Exodus 16:15), so Jesus Christ was the living manna, the Bread of Life sent down from heaven, as Jesus himself testified. Note how he linked himself to Moses:

"Then Jesus said unto them, Verily, verily, I say unto you, Moses gave you not that bread from heaven; but my Father giveth you the true bread from heaven.

"For the bread of God is he which cometh down from heaven, and giveth life unto the world. . . .

"And Jesus said unto them, I am the bread of life: he that cometh to me shall never hunger; and he that believeth on me shall never thirst. . . .

"Verily, verily, I say unto you, He that believeth on me hath everlasting life.

"I am that bread of life.

"Your fathers did eat manna in the wilderness, and are dead.

"This is the bread which cometh down from heaven, that a man may eat thereof, and not die" (John 6:32–50).

Just as Moses was the mediator of the Old Covenant, so Jesus Christ was the Mediator of the New Covenant (Hebrews 8:5–6; 9:15–24; 12:24).

Just as Moses saved and redeemed his people from oppression, death, and destruction, so Jesus Christ did the same for his people. Elder Bruce R. McConkie wrote: "Moses delivered Israel from Egypt, from bondage, from the lash, from abject and hopeless slavery, from a state in which they were physically oppressed and spiritually sick; and then for forty years he led them through a wasted wilderness, schooling and training the while, that they might finally be prepared for their promised land. Christ, the Great Deliverer, offers freedom to all who are under the bondage of sin and leads them through the wilderness of life to an Eternal Promised Land, where they will be free forever from the slavery of sin and the oppression of unrighteousness."[3]

There are many other ways in which Moses paralleled and prefigured the life and ministry of Jesus Christ. Both are judges, lawgivers, and miracle workers, and it is clear that Moses understood that his roles were a similitude of the Messiah, the Lord Jesus Christ. More important, Jesus Christ left his witness that he, as the mortal Messiah, knew that Moses had been called and chosen to stand through the ages not only as his type and shadow but also as his second witness. As he said, "Do not think that I will accuse you to the Father: there is one that accuseth you, even Moses, in whom ye trust. For had ye believed Moses, ye would have believed me: for he wrote of me. But if ye believe not his writings, how shall ye believe my words?" (John 5:45–47).

JOSHUA

Even a cursory reading of the Old Testament reveals that Joshua, able successor to Moses, was also a similitude of Moses, and, hence, a similitude of Jesus Christ. Almost everything said about the ways in which Moses stands as a type and shadow of the Messiah is also true of Joshua. He was a lawgiver, a deliverer (spiritually and militarily), and a prophet. He stood in the presence of the Lord and, just like Moses, was told, "Loose thy shoe from off thy foot; for the place whereon thou standest is holy" (Joshua 5:15; compare Exodus 3:5).

Joshua was also given control of the waters, just as Moses and Jesus were (compare Joshua 3:13–17; Exodus 14:21–31; Mark 5:39–41). Joshua was magnified at the parting of the Jordan River just as Moses had been magnified by the Lord in the eyes of the people when the Red Sea was parted. The Lord promised Joshua, "This day will I begin to magnify thee in the sight of all Israel, that they may know that, as I was with Moses, so I will be with thee" (Joshua 3:7). As Joshua parted the waters of the Jordan and "all the Israelites passed over on dry ground" (Joshua 3:17), the promise began to be fulfilled. "On that day the Lord magnified Joshua in the sight of all Israel; and they feared him, as they feared Moses, all the days of his life" (Joshua 4:14).

But, as Joshua came to realize, the real lesson to be learned was that he stood in the place of the Lord. What Joshua did was really what the Lord did working through him—"that all the people of the earth might know the hand of the Lord, that it is mighty: that ye might fear the Lord your God for ever" (Joshua 4:24). Thus, Joshua was a similitude of the Lord in the truest sense, for his hand was the Lord's hand, according to the Lord's own decree.

Joshua did what he did through the same means "by which Moses brought the children of Israel through the Red Sea on dry ground" (D&C 8:3). It was through the Lord's power and plan. Both times Israel passed through water into a new life. Such symbolic association with the concept of baptism in the name of Christ is unmistakable. And what's more, Joshua, who led the people to a newness of life, bore the name by which the Messiah would be known while he sojourned in mortality. The name *Jesus* is the anglicized Greek form of the Hebrew name *Joshua* (or, more particularly, *Yeshua*). The Hebrew name *Yeshua* or *Yehoshua* literally means "Jehovah is salvation." Just as Christ is the salvation of all people in an eternal sense, so Joshua, son of Nun, was the salvation of his people in a temporal sense.

Joshua was the earthly commander-in-chief of the Israelite armies during the conquest of the promised land. He represented Jehovah and was a similitude of him—the heavenly battle master of his people throughout history. As Jehovah said to Moses and Joshua, "The Lord your God which goeth before you, he shall fight for you" (Deuteronomy 1:30; compare Joshua 10:14; 23:10).

Joshua's great achievement was his constancy in leading God's people. He was a judge, mediator, and beacon to them as they progressed toward an inspired destination. As a similitude of Christ, it may be said with perfect propriety that Joshua led God's people to the promised land as the Messiah leads the way to the eternal land of promise. The concept of being led to a land of promise as a type or shadow of the Messiah's mission was powerfully articulated in the Book of Mormon when Alma discussed the spiritual significance of the Liahona with his son Helaman: "And now I say, is there not a type in this thing? For just as surely as this director did bring our fathers, by following its course, to the promised land, shall the words of Christ, if we follow their course, carry us beyond this vale of sorrow into a far better land of promise" (Alma 37:45). Moses, Joshua, and Jesus were like each other in many profound ways. And they pointed to each other.

CHAPTER 8

BOAZ AND SAMUEL
TYPES AND SHADOWS IN THE REIGN OF THE JUDGES

The book of Ruth is a wonderful story of loyalty and love that is intricately tied to the Messiah. Its setting is Bethlehem (a Hebrew name which means "house of bread"), and the story occurs at a time when, ironically, there was no bread—a time of famine. Its heroine is an ancestress of Jesus of Nazareth who converted to the religion and people of Israel. These details alone are important, for in a place called the "house of bread," at a time when there was "no bread," the lineage of the Bread of Life was being strengthened by a convert to the covenant people. Ruth is the convert who becomes an ancestress of Jesus of Nazareth.

As the story opens, the family of Elimelech leaves Bethlehem because of the famine and goes to the land of Moab to live. Elimelech dies and his two sons marry Moabite women, but after ten years the sons die as well. Widowed and childless, Elimelech's wife, Naomi, plans to return to her homeland because the famine had abated. "Wherefore she went forth out of the place where she was, and her two daughters in law with her; and they went on the way to return unto the land of Judah" (Ruth 1:7). At this point Naomi turned to her widowed daughters-in-law and encouraged them to go back to their own mother's house. Naomi then blessed them, kissed them, and wept over them as she said good-bye.

But Ruth refused to leave. In a stunning declaration of loyalty, she proclaimed that her mother-in-law's covenants would now be her covenants and her mother-in-law's people would now be her people. "And Ruth said, Intreat me not to leave thee, or to return from following after thee: for whither thou goest, I will go; and where thou lodgest, I will lodge: thy people shall be my people, and thy God my God: Where thou diest, will I die, and there will I be buried: the Lord do so to me, and more also, if ought but death part thee and me. When she saw that she was stedfastly minded to go with her, then she left speaking unto her" (Ruth 1:16–18).

Few passages in the Old Testament match the beauty and emotive power of Ruth's profession of faith and commitment. Her virtue and strength of character are an example for the ages. But because Ruth had given up her former religion and her former life in order to unite with Israel, she had no place to turn. She strikingly exemplifies the truth, articulated by the Savior, that choosing to participate in the kingdom of God may separate individuals from their family, friends, and culture: "For I am come to set a man at variance against his father, and the daughter against her mother, and the daughter in law against her mother in law. . . . He that loveth father or mother more than me is not worthy of me: and he that loveth son or daughter more than me is not worthy of me" (Matthew 10:35–37). As Jesus says in this passage, he and his gospel require individuals to make choices, sometimes hard choices, and commitments to him over others. Membership in the Lord's family is decided not by blood or birth but by conformity to God's will through the covenant. Accordingly, if anyone sacrifices all in order to follow God, God will not leave any of his covenant family members without help. "But now the Lord saith, . . . them that honour me I will honour" (1 Samuel 2:30). He did not leave Ruth destitute or helpless. He provided a redeemer for her and Naomi and fulfilled a promise of temporal and spiritual redemption. The name of Ruth's and Naomi's redeemer was Boaz—who is a similitude of Jesus Christ.

Ruth and Naomi returned to Jerusalem at the time of the barley harvest. Perhaps under inspiration, Ruth gleaned in the fields of Boaz, who was a "mighty man of wealth" (Ruth 2:1) and a kinsman of Naomi's deceased husband. The ancient law of gleaning was a kind of welfare system. The Lord asked landowners to leave some produce in their fields to allow the needy, the fatherless, the widow, and the stranger the opportunity to harvest enough for their sustenance (Leviticus 19:9–10; 23:22; Deuteronomy 24:19–22). Ruth found favor with Boaz, who wanted to marry her if the nearest kinsman, to whom the right belonged according to the law in Deuteronomy 25:5–10, declined. He did decline and set the stage for one greater.

Boaz married Ruth and thus became a redeemer and savior of the two widows—a thinly veiled reflection of God's love and redemptive power. Without Boaz, both Naomi and Ruth would have remained on the fringes of society, devoid of meaningful status, security, voice, opportunities, or connectedness to a patriarchal culture that sometimes inadvertently, but wrongly, left widows and orphans powerless and alone. Boaz's gracious and beneficent actions reversed all of that, as the text indicates:

"And Boaz said unto the elders, and unto all the people, Ye are witnesses this day, that I have bought all that was

Elimelech's, and all that was Chilion's and Mahlon's, of the hand of Naomi.

"Morever Ruth the Moabitess, the wife of Mahlon, have I *purchased* to be my wife, to raise up the name of the dead upon his inheritance, that the name of the dead be not cut off from among his brethren, and from the gate of his place: ye are witnesses of this day. . . .

"So Boaz took Ruth, and she was his wife: and when he went in unto her, the Lord gave her conception, and she bare a son.

"And the women said unto Naomi, Blessed be the Lord, which hath not left thee this day without a *kinsman,* that his name may be famous in Israel" (Ruth 4:9–14; emphasis added).

The Hebrew word used to describe Boaz in this passage, which the King James Version translates as "kinsman," is *go'el.* This word translates literally as "redeemer." The King James translators probably did not recognize the deeper significance of the story nor the similitude of Christ inherent in the levirate law of Deuteronomy 25. Thus, they translated *go'el* as kinsman or next of kin. The levirate law (so called from Latin, *levir,* "husband's brother") is itself a typifying of Christ in that it asks that a deceased man's brother or kinsman stand in the place of the deceased, to provide for the needs of the widow, to rescue the family from any difficulty, and to raise up children in the name of the deceased brother. Thus, the deceased man's brother or kinsman was performing a substitutionary act, a vicarious service that the deceased man could not do for himself. Is this not the essence of the Lord's atonement?

Boaz was a redeemer in that he returned the widow Ruth to her former status as wife. She was no longer a disenfranchised member of society or the family of Israel. She had been purchased with a price. Likewise, all humanity, especially members of the covenant family, have a redeemer who has purchased or "bought [us] with a price" as Paul said—which price is his precious blood (1 Corinthians 6:20; Acts 20:28). The great Redeemer is Jesus Christ. The words of the chief apostle, Peter, also come to mind: "Forasmuch as ye know that ye were not redeemed with corruptible things . . . but with the precious blood of Christ, as of a lamb without blemish and without spot: who verily was foreordained before the foundation of the world, but was manifest in these last times for you" (1 Peter 1:18–20).

Ruth's redemption had everlasting consequences for the whole human family. The son of Boaz and Ruth was Obed, who was the father of Jesse, who was the father of David, through whose lineage came the royal Messiah, Jesus of Nazareth.

Truly, Boaz is a similitude of the Messiah, a truth which the story of Ruth was deliberately intended to portray. In the place called the "house of bread" would later come the "Bread of Life," the Savior, the Redeemer, who himself came into the world through a lineage that owed its origins to a literal earthly *go'el* or redeemer—Boaz.

There were many individuals during the period of the judges (the backdrop of Ruth's story) whose lives, or aspects of their lives, pointed to, mirrored, or foreshadowed the life of the Messiah, Jesus of Nazareth. Indeed, the position or role of judge itself, held by thirteen men and women between the death of Joshua and the coronation of King Saul (approximately two hundred years), is a type and similitude of him who was to come in the meridian of time.

Judges were lawgivers, civil officers who adjudicated cases

among the people, enforcers of God's will and laws, and, above all, military leaders and deliverers from distress and oppression brought on by Israel's enemies. Just as Jesus represented his Father to the people, Israel's judges were supposed to represent God to their people. Thus, Israel's judges were also intercessors on behalf of their people, as was Jesus Christ. Hence, faith in God was a key to the judges' success. The story of the judges, told in the book of Judges, recounts the cycle of Israel's rebellion against God and their alienation from him, a subsequent period of oppression, and then deliverance at the hands of the judges: Othniel (Judges 3:11), Ehud (3:30), Shamgar (3:31), Deborah (5:31), Gideon (8:28), Abimelech (9:22), Tola (10:2), Jair (10:3), Jephthah (12:7), Ibzan (12:9), Elon (12:1), Abdon (12:13), and Samson (15:20; 16:31).

The life and works of Israel's greatest earthly judge, however, are discussed not in the book of Judges but in a separate book bearing his name: Samuel. Not only was he judge of Israel but also a mighty prophet, performing priestly functions and offering sacrifices at various locations under the authority of the Melchizedek Priesthood, which he held.[1] After the selection of Israel's first king, Saul, Samuel appears to have ceased to function as judge, but he continued to function as prophet and priest and Jehovah's unequivocal representative and spokesman on earth. Though several episodes in Samuel's life foreshadow the coming of the Great Judge, Jesus Christ, one of particular importance parallels events surrounding the births of both Jesus and John the Baptist.

THE NATIVITY FORESHADOWED

Samuel's mother, Hannah, had no children for years. After an especially difficult period of time, she went to the house of the Lord to pray and seek comfort. The Lord heard her earnest pleas and blessed her with conception. She bore a son, whom she named Samuel: "His name is God." Aspects of this well-known story point us to the circumstances of the birth of the Messiah and of his cousin John. Thus, the story of Hannah foreshadows the story of the Nativity.

> Hannah went to the house of the Lord, seeking for, even struggling for, the blessing of posterity (1 Samuel 1:9–18). This too was the experience of Zacharias, who went to the Temple and whose prayer was heard after he struggled for, wrestled for, the blessing of posterity (Luke 1:13). Said the Prophet Joseph Smith: "The priesthood was given to Aaron and his posterity throughout all generations. We can trace the lineage down to Zacharias, he being the only lawful administrator in his day. And the Jews knew it well, for they always acknowledged the priesthood. Zacharias, having no children, knew that the promise of God must fail. Consequently, he went into the temple to wrestle with God, according to the order of the priesthood, to obtain a promise of a son."[2]

> Hannah referred to herself as the handmaid of the Lord, just as Mary, the mother of Jesus, referred to herself as the handmaid of the Lord (1 Samuel 1:11; Luke 1:48).

> Both Samuel and Jesus were foreordained in premortality to come to earth when they did. "The miraculous circumstances surrounding the birth and the call of Samuel make it clear that he had a divine calling before he entered mortality, and that he was chosen to play an important role in the history of Israel."[3]

The blessing of having posterity, a son of promise, caused Hannah to rejoice through a great psalm of praise. Likewise, the blessing of bearing a son of promise, even the Son of God, caused Mary to offer a great psalm of praise, known as the "Magnificat." The birth of a son caused Zacharias to utter a psalm of praise and prophecy, known as the "Benedictus" by Christians throughout the world (compare 1 Samuel 1:1–10; Luke 1:46–55; Luke 1:67–79). Hannah's psalm is even believed to be the model for Mary's "Magnificat."

The language of Hannah's psalm bears marked similarities to the language of Mary's poetic song and Zacharias's psalm:

Hannah: "My heart rejoiceth in the Lord" (1 Samuel 2:1). Mary: "My spirit hath rejoiced in God my Saviour" (Luke 1:47).

Hannah: "Mine horn is exalted in the Lord" (1 Samuel 2:1). Zacharias: "[The Lord] hath raised up an horn of salvation" (Luke 1:69).

Hannah: "The Lord maketh poor, and maketh rich: he bringeth low, and lifteth up. He raiseth up the poor out of the dust" (1 Samuel 2:7–8). Mary: "[God] hath put down the mighty from their seats, and exalted them of low degree" (Luke 1:52).

Lastly, Hannah's psalm of praise anticipated the coming of Jesus Christ in other specific, impressive ways. Hannah recognized him as the "rock," as the Judge—"by him actions are weighed," and as the Lord of resurrection—"[he] killeth, and maketh alive: he bringeth down to the grave, and bringeth up" (1 Samuel 2:2, 3, 6).

Not only was Samuel a similitude of Jesus Christ but Hannah was herself a similitude of the mother of the Lord and the parents of John the Baptist. She spoke the words her successors—Mary and Zacharias—would speak, and she prophesied in poetic language of the many aspects of the Savior's mortal mission and ministry, especially the Atonement, just as Mary and Zacharias would do. Hannah declared that through the Lord's power, all "the adversaries of the Lord [would] be broken to pieces." The Lord would "judge the ends of the earth," and he would "exalt the horn [the power, strength, and capacity] of his anointed" (1 Samuel 2:10). That is, the Lord would strengthen and endow with power his servants, his anointed, who were themselves types and similitudes of the Anointed One. For Hannah, one of the Lord's anointed was her own son, Samuel, who was in the similitude of the Lord she worshiped—the Lord to come (1 Samuel 1:11; 2:18; 3:1–21). Samuel's years of preparatory service in the house of the Lord, as arranged by his mother, show that both Hannah and Samuel knew who it was to whom Samuel belonged. Those years also endowed Samuel with the powers he would use to bless others and to minister as Jesus himself ministered.

As a similitude of Jesus Christ, Samuel prophesied of the Savior and thus received special mention by Peter, the chief apostle, and by the Savior himself. Speaking to the Jews in the Temple, Peter said that "all the prophets *from Samuel* and those that follow after, as many as have spoken, have likewise foretold of these days" (Acts 3:24; emphasis added). This same declaration was made by the resurrected Jesus to the Nephites: "Verily I say unto you, yea, and all the prophets from Samuel and those that follow after, as many as have spoken, have testified of me" (3 Nephi 20:24).

Samuel was regarded as one of the greatest of the prophets by the Jews of the meridian dispensation because he was thought to have been the last individual to hold the official offices of both judge and prophet before the establishment of the Israelite monarchy. Paul alluded to this when he said that God gave the people of Israel judges "until Samuel the prophet" (Acts 13:20). As a prophet, not only was Samuel himself an anointed one but he sought out and anointed others, including the first two kings of Israel—Saul and David (1 Samuel 9:16; 15:1; 16:13). All of this was in similitude and imitation of the Anointed One, Jesus of Nazareth. In his role as judge, Samuel foreshadowed the coming of Jesus and the Atonement since Israel's judges acted as intercessors—Jesus being the Great Intercessor (Isaiah 53:12; Romans 8:34; 2 Nephi 2:9; Mosiah 14:12; 15:8). "The great power of Samuel as an intercessor is recalled in the Psalms, where he is regarded along with Moses and Aaron as one who was able to cry unto the Lord and be heard (Psalms 99:6), and by Jeremiah, who pointedly indicted Israel with the declaration of the Lord that 'though Moses and Samuel stood before me, yet my mind could not be toward this people' (Jeremiah 15:1)."[4] Samuel—as prophet, priest, anointed one, temple officiator, judge, anointer of others, and ruler of Israel—was a type and shadow of Jesus Christ.

CHAPTER 9

DAVID AND SOLOMON
FATHERS OF THE ROYAL LINE

King David is *the* prototype of an earthly royal messiah or "anointed one." He is usually regarded as Israel's greatest monarch and was anointed king by two of Israel's prophets: Samuel (1 Samuel 16:13) and Nathan (2 Samuel 12:7). He established a religiously grounded kingdom and subdued Israel's enemies under his feet. Thus, he was a powerful type and foreshadowing of Jesus Christ, who will come at the end of days and conquer all of God's enemies. In truth, all earthly rulers are only imitations of the Great King-Messiah, as Joseph Smith was told: "Wherefore, be subject unto the powers that be, until he reigns whose right it is to reign, and subdues all enemies under his feet" (D&C 58:22).

From its beginning, David's life pointed to One greater. Like Jesus, David was born in Bethlehem (1 Samuel 16:1; Luke 2:4–7), an important harbinger of the appearance of the Messiah, who, it was prophesied, would come from Bethlehem (Micah 5:2). Like Jesus, David was from the tribe of Judah. Like Jesus, David was a shepherd (1 Samuel 16:11–12, 19), although Jesus is the Good Shepherd, Shepherd of the Father's flock, and the Shepherd of our souls (1 Peter 2:25). Jesus testified of his own shepherding role in memorable fashion: "I am the good shepherd, and know my sheep, and am known of mine. As the Father knoweth me, even so know I the Father: and I lay down my life for the sheep. And other sheep I have, which are not of this fold: them also I must bring, and they shall hear my voice; and there shall be one fold, and one shepherd" (John 10:14–16). David was very much like Jesus in the kind of care he exercised with his sheep.

Even today we see shepherds whose care of their flocks reminds us of the care with which the Savior and David discharged their own similar responsibilities. While living in the Holy Land, my family and I went with some students one afternoon to the fields just north of Bethlehem to read and ponder the scriptures related to Jesus' life. As the sun set and the church bells of Bethlehem tolled in the background, a modern-day Bedouin shepherd led his flock right past our group as we perched on some rocks. Cameras were whipped out of their bags, and flashbulbs lit the darkening sky.

One straggler, a cute little lamb who seemed to be paying no attention to the others, lagged far behind the rest of the flock. When the rest of the flock passed by our group and went down over the hill out of sight, the little straggler became confused, then agitated, and then frightened—unsure about which way to go to find the flock. Flashbulbs again lit the sky, adding to the terror of the little lamb. All of a sudden, from down over the hill, came the voice of the shepherd, though he remained out of view. The little lamb's ears perked up as he ran toward the voice of the shepherd, and he was soon cradled in his master's arms. Both went down the hill together, rejoicing, as the shepherd continued to speak soothing words to the once-lost lamb. I will never forget that image. Truly, the sheep know the voice of the shepherd.

As a shepherd, David possessed great courage and tenacity. In the discharge of his stewardship, he slew a lion and a bear and demonstrated that he, like Jesus, was willing to lay down his life for his sheep—an important foreshadowing of Jesus' own teachings and example (1 Samuel 17:34–36). Ultimately, his courage fortified him at the time of Israel's great hour of distress caused by Goliath, the giant from Gath. David slew Goliath and showed that strength and success are a function of trust in God and righteous living (1 Samuel 17:37–58). In parallel spiritual fashion, Jesus slew the giants of sin and death, showing that his strength came from his Father and his sinless life.

David was the great-grandson of Boaz, himself a significant harbinger and similitude of the Redeemer. David's early life was a preparation for his redemptive role as Israel's warrior-king, conqueror, and bringer of political and military salvation to Israel. In truth, his reign "was the most brilliant" of Israelite history. David was a gatherer and a uniter. He united the factious tribes of Israel into a nation. He secured Israel's undisputed possession of the Holy Land and expanded Israel's borders. He established Jerusalem as the capital of the united monarchy and seat of his throne as king, thus foreshadowing the coming of the Great King, Jesus Christ, during the meridian of time as well as the Millennium. During that thousand years of peace, Christ will reign personally on the earth from both Old and New Jerusalem (Isaiah 2:3). Finally, David established the government of the kingdom of Israel on the foundation of the religion of Jehovah so that the will of God was the law of the land. For these reasons, David's reign was later regarded as the nation's golden age and the type and similitude of the more glorious age when the Messiah would come (Isaiah 16:4; Jeremiah 23:5; Ezekiel 37:24–28).[1]

Clearly, "David personified Yahweh's [Jehovah's] reign over Judah and, by extension, Israel."[2] Therefore, he also personified (during his righteous days) Christ's reign over all of the Father's children. Not insignificantly, David's name means "beloved." This is also a type, pointing us to Jesus who was the Beloved of the Father (Matthew 3:17; 17:5; 2 Peter 1:17). David was a poet, a musician, and a deeply spiritual person. Indeed, he was a man after the Lord's own heart (1 Samuel 13:13–14)—again, a true similitude of Jesus Christ.

Just as David pointed forward to Jesus Christ, so Jesus pointed back to David and acknowledged that He was the fulfillment of David's role as a type and shadow. By divine appointment and foreordination, Jesus was born into the lineage of David, in the city of David, to fulfill messianic prophecies and expectations. Elder McConkie noted: "No single concept was more firmly lodged in the minds of the Jews in Jesus' day than the universal belief that their Messiah would be the Son of David. They expected him to come and reign on David's throne. They looked for a temporal deliverer who would throw off the yoke of Roman bondage and make Israel free again. They sought a ruler who would restore that glory and worldwide influence and prestige which was enjoyed when the Son of Jesse sat on Israel's throne."[3]

Several passages of scripture attest that the Messiah was expected to be the Son of David, through the Davidic royal line. King David himself was the first to receive the prophetic word that one of his posterity would be Israel's Eternal King: "And when thy days be fulfilled, and thou shalt sleep with thy fathers, I will set up thy seed after thee, which shall proceed out of thy bowels, and I will establish his kingdom. He shall build an house for my name, and I will stablish the throne of his kingdom for ever" (2 Samuel 7:12–13). As noted by Elder McConkie, "In substance and thought content Gabriel reaffirmed this same truth to Mary when he said in Luke 1:33, 'And he shall reign over the house of Jacob for ever; and of his kingdom there shall be no end.'"[4]

The Gospel author Matthew begins his book (his testimony) with a genealogy that is intended "to prove that Jesus is the rightful Messiah according to Jewish law by showing his descent from Abraham, and from David and the kings of Judah . . . that Jesus was 'son of David' through Joseph."[5] As heir of David, Jesus demonstrated one more evidence of his messiahship (see Acts 2:29–36; the apocryphal Psalms of Solomon 17:23). Though earlier Jews did not universally hold that the Messiah was the Son of David, that belief became standard Jewish doctrine after 63 B.C. when the Roman general Pompey conquered Jerusalem. From then on, the Jews constantly sought freedom from the yoke of Roman overlordship, and the promise of a messianic deliverer, in the mold and lineage of King David, was their greatest hope.

During the last week of his mortal ministry, Jesus asked the Pharisees, "What think ye of Christ [the Anointed One]? whose son is he? They say unto him, The son of David" (Matthew 22:42). Here Jesus was asking not what the Pharisees thought of himself (Jesus) but what conception they had of the office and person of the Messiah. Their answer was straightforward, but it did not encompass the concept of a Messiah as we, today, understand it. By that point in history, the most important concepts associated with the Messiah—"deliverance from spiritual darkness, of being freed from the bondage of sin, of a kingdom which is not of this world . . . all made possible through an infinite and eternal atonement"—was lost doctrine, unknown to most Jews.[6] The Pharisees "hoped for a Messiah who would overthrow the Roman conqueror and inaugurate a prosperous Jewish state."[7]

Of course, Jesus of Nazareth fits every conception, every aspect, of the true Messiah, but his first and greatest conquest at his first coming was not the conquest of the Romans but his destruction of sin, sorrow, and death. To emphasize this point, Jesus rode into Jerusalem during his Triumphal Entry on a donkey, the ancient symbol of Jewish royalty and peace.[8] But when he comes again, he will be riding a white horse, symbol of war and conquest in the ancient world, as John testified: "And I saw heaven opened, and behold a white horse; and he that sat upon him was called Faithful and True, and in righteousness he doth judge and make war. His eyes were as a flame of fire, and on his head were many crowns; and he had a name written, that no man knew, but he himself" (Revelation 19:11–12). Jesus wears every crown. But the most impressive symbols of his power and authority depicted in scripture hark back to his inextricable link with the power and authority of Israel's second king. Jesus is "he that hath the key of David" (Revelation 3:7). Jesus is "the Root of David" (Revelation 5:5). Jesus is "the offspring of David" (Revelation 22:16). Ultimately, "the kingdoms of this world are become the kingdoms of our Lord, and of his Christ; and he shall reign for ever and ever" (Revelation 11:15).

SOLOMON

Solomon was the son of David and Bathsheba (2 Samuel 12:24) and was designated by his father to succeed him as king of Israel (1 Kings 1:1–53). Solomon was also a type and similitude of Jesus Christ. Solomon's name literally means "his peace." Jesus was the "Prince of Peace," who said to his followers, "My peace I give unto you" (John 14:27). As a "son of David," Solomon was the first to bear, as his name, the title of peace that Jesus Christ bore, which identified him with the expected Messiah. Solomon, like Jesus, was the son of a king who himself became a king, even though there were those who opposed his coming to the throne.

David charged Solomon to walk in the ways of the Lord (1 Kings 2:1–9), and for a time he did so. "Solomon loved the Lord, walking in the statutes of David his father" (1 Kings 3:3). Solomon's statutes were David's statutes, which were the Lord's statutes. In Gibeon, the Lord appeared to Solomon and blessed him with his request—great wisdom, discernment, and judgment—so that there was none like unto Solomon among all the kings of the earth (1 Kings 3:5–13). Perhaps the most famous example of Solomon's wisdom, judgment, justice, and fairness was his disposition of the case involving two women who claimed to be the mother of a young child. Solomon commanded that the child be divided in half, and his sword of justice was brought forward. But before the action was carried out, the real mother asked that the other woman be given the living child in order to spare his life. Solomon then knew who the real mother was (1 Kings 3:16–28). Solomon, the righteous judge, was like the Great Judge, Jesus Christ, whose word of judgment is like a sword, "quick and powerful, sharper than a two-edged sword, to the dividing asunder of both joints and marrow" (D&C 11:2; 12:2; 14:2; 33:1).

Perhaps Solomon's greatest accomplishment was his building of the Jerusalem Temple, often called Solomon's Temple, which was the house of the Lord. Solomon's "house" was the Lord's house. Jesus spoke of the Temple in his day as "my house" (Matthew 21:13). Not only was Solomon of old a similitude of Jesus Christ with regard to the Temple, but it is in temples, houses of the Lord, that modern disciples of the Lord can go to receive the ultimate blessings that allow them to become just like the Lord, to receive the fulness of the priesthood, to become princes (princesses) of peace themselves, and to inherit all that the Lord possesses (Romans 8:14–17; D&C 84:33–38).

CHAPTER 10

ELIJAH AND ELISHA
POWER OVER THE ELEMENTS

As we have seen, pairs of patriarchs or prophets sometimes show much in common with each other. Not only do they reinforce the principles taught by the other but together fulfill the ancient law of witnesses, especially when it comes to testifying of the Messiah and pointing to him. The lives and ministries of Elijah and Elisha are that way. These two powerful prophets in Israel resembled and paralleled each other as they also typified and foreshadowed the life of Christ.

Yet the lives of Elijah and Elisha started out very differently. Elijah was a country boy. He grew up in the solitary hill country of Gilead. Elisha lived in cities. Elijah seems to have possessed a kind of fiery zeal, and his forceful deeds scarcely have an equal in terms of their "dramatic manifestations and the visible exhibition of divine power."[1] On the other hand, Elisha was possessed of a gentle, kind, affectionate, merciful disposition, which characterizes many of his miracles.[2] But Elisha became the attendant and disciple of Elijah and eventually his successor as prophet, and his activities sometimes looked like carbon copies of his mentor's.

For example, Elijah's last miracle, smiting the waters of the

Jordan River with his mantle, was performed just before he was taken into heaven in a chariot of fire: "And Elijah took his mantle and wrapped it together, and smote the waters, and they were divided hither and thither, so that they two went over on dry ground" (2 Kings 2:8). This was also the first recorded miracle of Elisha's prophetic ministry: "And he took the mantle of Elijah that fell from him, and smote the waters, and said, Where is the Lord God of Elijah? And when he also had smitten the waters, they parted hither and thither: and Elisha went over" (2 Kings 2:14).

This episode is significant for at least five reasons. First, Elisha's miracle came right after he asked for "a double portion" of his master's spirit (2 Kings 2:9). The parallel miracles show that the student had inherited the prophetic powers of his master. Second, Elijah's mantle (shawl), which fell on Elisha, became a term synonymous with prophetic succession, "the mantle of the prophet." Third, after Elijah performed his miracle and was taken up, Elisha cried, "My father, my father, the chariot of Israel" (2 Kings 2:12). Elijah was more than just a teacher to Elisha; he was a true mentor, engendering in his disciple great affection for himself and for the things of righteousness. Fourth, the two miracles of Elijah and Elisha bear a striking resemblance to the mighty acts performed by other powerful prophets—namely, Moses and Joshua, each of whom smote the waters before him and crossed over on "dry ground" (Exodus 14:22, 24; Joshua 3:17). Fifth, and most important, the miracles of Elijah and Elisha in controlling the waters and other elements pointed to Jesus Christ and were in similitude of him who also had control over the waters and over the elements (compare Matthew 14:22–33; Mark 4:41).

Those mighty prophets who possessed the keys of the

sealing powers of the priesthood have had control over the elements of the heavens and the earth. Elijah sealed shut the heavens and commanded the elements so that there was neither dew nor rain for years (1 Kings 17:1). Elisha sealed the heavens to fulfill the Lord's purposes (2 Kings 3:17). Nephi, son of Helaman, also sealed the heavens and brought about famine in the land in order to bring about the Lord's purposes among his children (Helaman 10:7; 11:4–6, 17). President J. Reuben Clark, a counselor in the First Presidency from 1933 to 1961, explained that the priesthood has been and will continue to be "the greatest power and force that there is in the world. That power and that force when understood and exercised, involves the control of all the elements that go to make up the universe; compared to that power and that control the H-bomb is a mere tiny firecracker."[3] Elder Bruce R. McConkie also said that one of the ultimate blessings that will come to righteous priesthood holders is that they will "have power to govern all things, both temporal and spiritual, the kingdoms of the world and the elements and storms and powers of the earth."[4]

Possessing power over the elements of the earth, Elijah and Elisha each multiplied a widow's food supply so that each woman could sustain her family (1 Kings 17:10–16; 2 Kings 4:1–7). In the case of the miracle Elijah performed, the Lord instructed him to go to Zarephath to have the widow feed him during the period of severe famine caused by Elijah's sealing of the heavens. The poor widow possessed only enough flour to make a small bread-cake. And yet Elijah asked her to feed him. The prophet's request was not an act of selfishness, however, but rather a test of the woman's faith. Because of her faith and unselfishness, Elijah promised the widow that her barrel of flour and her container of oil would not become depleted for the duration of the famine.

So great a lesson did this woman's actions teach that Jesus used the story to try to dispel the faithlessness and spiritual darkness rampant among those of his own hometown. "And he said, Verily I say unto you, No prophet is accepted in his own country. But I tell you of a truth, many widows were in Israel in the days of Elias [Elijah], when the heaven was shut up three years and six months, when great famine was throughout all the land; but unto none of them was Elias sent, save unto Sarepta, a city of Sidon, unto a woman that was a widow" (Luke 4:24–26).

Jesus was identifying himself with Elijah. He was saying, in effect, that he was doing what Elijah did, but the famine he was facing was spiritual. As the Messiah and Son of God, his power was like that of Elijah, only much greater, to bless the lives of his countrymen. But they rejected him and his power and therefore, like Elijah, he would go to others. To make sure they got the message, Jesus then invoked the example of Elisha (even in Jesus' mind Elijah and Elisha went together): "And many lepers were in Israel in the time of Eliseus [Elisha] the prophet, and none of them was cleansed, saving Naaman the Syrian" (Luke 4:27).

Of this episode, Elder Bruce R. McConkie said: "How aptly Jesus chose his illustrations! Both of these ancient prophets, dishonored by their own, conferred great blessings upon foreigners. So it was with the Nazarenes; others, not they, had seen his great works."[5]

Jesus was teaching here that both Elijah and Elisha were types and similitudes of himself, the Messiah. Like himself, Elijah and Elisha were rejected and, in a direct reference to

Naaman, the Syrian general who was healed of leprosy by Elisha, Jesus indicated that such healings and miracles could only happen when an individual possessed faith and humility (2 Kings 5). In cleansing Naaman, Elisha foreshadowed or acted in the similitude of Jesus, who cleansed many lepers (Matthew 8:2–4; Mark 1:40–45; Luke 5:12–15; 17:11–15).

This remarkable miracle of Elisha's was a similitude of Christ in other ways. Leprosy, the horrible decay of flesh and cartilage in a living human, was symbolic of religious impurity, sin, and death. Those afflicted with leprosy were considered "unclean" and were segregated or cut off from the rest of the people. The manner in which Naaman was cleansed pointed to the way in which all those afflicted with "spiritual uncleanness," and sin may be cleansed. Naaman, a Syrian, had to humble himself and bathe in the living waters of the Jordan, the waters designated by Israel's prophet. Likewise, all those seeking spiritual cleansing must come unto Jesus, who is the Living Water. They must be immersed in the waters designated by the prophets—the waters of baptism—which are also living water (John 4:10–14; 6:35; 7:37; Alma 42:27; Revelation 21:6; 22:1, 17).

There are other examples of Elijah and Elisha performing the miracles that Jesus performed. In an episode foreshadowing two of Christ's greatest miracles, Elisha fed one hundred men with only twenty loaves and had food left over (2 Kings 4:42–44). Jesus, of course, performed even more dramatic miracles of this type when he fed five thousand men (besides women and children) with five loaves and two fishes and had food left over, as all four Gospels relate (Matthew 14:14–21; Mark 6:34–44; Luke 9:11–17; John 6:3–14). A short time later, Jesus fed a multitude of four thousand with seven loaves and a few fishes (Matthew 15:32–38; Mark 8:1–9).

Both Elijah and Elisha used their power to raise the dead. Elisha raised a woman's son in much the same way as Elijah had when he raised the widow's son (compare 1 Kings 17:21–22 and 2 Kings 4:32–35). Both prophets showed great compassion, and, significantly, did what Jesus would do centuries later. Elijah and Jesus raised sons of widowed mothers, which is especially touching. Raising the dead, especially the widow's son in the village of Nain (Luke 7:11–17), was graphic testimony of Jesus' divine power (compare also Mark 5:41–44 and John 11:41–46). Although all prophets who have raised the dead have acted in similitude of the Savior, "none ever acted with such awesome majesty as the Lord Jesus, who, stopping the funeral cortege, said with simplicity: 'Young man, I say unto thee, Arise.'"[6]

The names of Elijah and Elisha complemented each other and pointed to Jesus Christ. Elijah means "Jehovah is my God." Elisha means either "God of salvation," or "God shall save." Both Elijah and Elisha, like Jesus, prophesied the future and constantly inveighed against the idolatry of Israel.

The resemblances between the ministries of Elijah, Elisha, and Jesus are attested in the New Testament. In fact, the actions of Jesus so much seemed to resemble the actions of the ancient prophet Elijah, and so much did the powerful personality of Jesus recall traditions about Elijah, that Jesus was thought to *be* Elijah returned. The most famous episode evincing this undercurrent of Jewish sentiment in Jesus' day occurred at Caesarea Philippi when Jesus asked his apostles who people said he was. "And they said, Some say that thou art . . . Elias [Elijah]" (Matthew 16:14).

Of course, Elijah was prophesied to return to earth, which he did, and this too was a similitude of the Messiah, Jesus Christ, and was done in preparation for His return, as Latter-day Saints know (Malachi 4:5–6; D&C 110). So important is Elijah's return, as outlined in scripture and tradition, that the Jewish people leave a seat vacant and open their doors during Passover so that Elijah may come in and hasten the arrival of the Messiah. Even to them Elijah, one of the greatest prophets of their history, is a foreshadowing and harbinger of the Messiah.

CHAPTER 11

HEZEKIAH

DELIVERER OF JERUSALEM

Hezekiah was a Davidic king, anointed in similitude of the Anointed One to fulfill his responsibilities in leading Judah righteously and delivering them from their enemies. His name means "Jehovah strengthens" or "Jehovah is strength." Hezekiah was one of the most important temporal rulers in the history of Israel.

The life of Hezekiah dramatically validates the Lord's declaration that he delivers his people from all their enemies and prospers them when they honor him (2 Kings 17:39; 18:11–12). Almost immediately upon ascending the throne, righteous Hezekiah, unlike his wicked father, Ahaz, enjoyed the constant help of the Lord. Thus, Hezekiah prospered in all he did (2 Chronicles 32:21; 2 Kings 18:7). He became Judah's earthly deliverer and acted in similitude of the great Deliverer, Jesus Christ. Hezekiah's righteous rule was a repudiation of all that his wicked father had stood for. His twenty-nine-year reign (715–687 B.C.) was such that the author of 2 Kings 18 ranked him as the greatest king Judah had ever known or ever would know (2 Kings 18:3–5). In fact, Chronicles devotes more attention to Hezekiah than any other king since

Solomon, including three chapters dedicated to his good deeds and inspired leadership (2 Chronicles 29–31).

At the heart of the Chronicler's admiration for Hezekiah's rule was the monarch's religious reform and restoration. Acting as a prophet of restoration after a period of apostasy, he modeled the life and deeds of Jesus, who is also called a prophet of restoration by John the Revelator (JST John 1:22–28). Numerous parallels in Chronicles between Hezekiah and the great king Solomon suggest that the Chronicler viewed Hezekiah as a "second Solomon." Wasting no time (beginning in the very first month of his reign, as the text says), Hezekiah reopened, repaired, and repurified the temple (2 Chronicles 29:3, 15–19). These actions foreshadowed the Savior's attempts to reform the Jerusalem Temple (John 2:13–17; Matthew 21:12–16). Hezekiah revitalized the Levites and Aaronic priests and reestablished proper sacrificial worship (2 Chronicles 29:4–12, 20–36). Last but not least, Hezekiah decreed a Passover celebration that sought to bring together all the tribes of Israel for the first time since Solomon's days (2 Chronicles 30). He believed there was great power in unified righteousness and in focusing on the apex of temple ordinances.

Following through with the parallel to Solomon, the Chronicler subtly mentioned the rewards of Hezekiah's loyalty to Jehovah: wealth (2 Chronicles 32:27–29), magnified respect in the eyes of all the gentile nations (2 Chronicles 32:23), and an expanded dominion—much more than his recent predecessors had experienced (2 Chronicles 30–25). All of these were also enjoyed by Solomon in his righteous days.

Hezekiah's reforms, which focused on the Temple and the ordinance (Passover) that most clearly pointed to Christ's atonement, engendered in the people of Judah far more righteousness than had existed for several years. Hezekiah explained to the priests and Levites that the Lord's past anger against Judah (and hence their political and social woes) were traceable to their forefathers' defilement of God's holy house (2 Chronicles 29:6–9). The message, therefore, seems clear for every group in every dispensation which has placed itself in a covenant relationship to God through temple ordinances: community well-being depends on purity and exactness in temple worship (2 Chronicles 29:10–11). This was the thrust of Jesus' instruction, as he himself was found daily teaching in the Temple (Matthew 26:55).

Upon the death of Sargon II in 705 B.C., Hezekiah decided to break altogether from the grasp of Assyria (2 Kings 18:7). In 701 B.C., Sargon's son Sennacherib invaded Judah with a huge army to crush the rebellion. Before approaching Jerusalem, he attacked and conquered all the other fortified cities of Judah (2 Kings 18:13). Things looked bleak for Hezekiah (2 Kings 18:13–16). But he faced the challenge as an inspired deliverer. He consulted with his advisers to carry out his life-saving plans. "In all his righteous efforts, including his military undertakings to restore and preserve the kingdom, Hezekiah had as his constant ally and advisor the prophet Isaiah."[1] The fortifications of the city were repaired, and a secret tunnel (now commonly called Hezekiah's Tunnel) was dug through solid rock to carry into the city the waters of the Gihon Spring, which bubbled up in the Kidron Valley outside the city walls (2 Kings 20:20; 2 Chronicles 32:4, 30).

As the systematic destruction of the kingdom of Judah reached a crescendo under the Assyrian onslaught, Hezekiah encouraged his military commanders with a message of comfort and courage: "Be strong and courageous, be not afraid nor dismayed for the king of Assyria, nor for all the multitude that is with him: *for there be more with us than with him:* with him is an arm of flesh; but with us is the Lord our God to help us, and to fight our battles" (2 Chronicles 32:7–8; emphasis added). The account in 2 Kings reports that Hezekiah also made a bid for peace. He sent tribute to the Assyrian king encamped at Lachish in an attempt to induce the Assyrians to go home. While it is likely that we do not have the whole story, it appears that Hezekiah also sent tribute as a way of stalling for time to complete the last of his preparations for defense against an expected siege.

Hezekiah's tribute payment hardly satisfied Sennacherib. He sent two officials, his army commander and his chief chamberlain, to intimidate and humiliate both the leaders and the people of Judah into submission. They said, in effect, "We have already destroyed other lands; we have already destroyed your territory; you are the last to hold out. Your feeble god cannot possibly deliver you, just as the gods of other lands could not deliver them. Give up and resign yourselves to the inevitable" (see 2 Kings 18:17–35).

Hezekiah turned to what he knew was Judah's only salvation—the Lord. He himself went to the temple and concurrently sent messengers to the prophet Isaiah (2 Kings 19:1–5). The Lord's word through his prophet was one of assurance: "Be not afraid" (2 Kings 19:6). In fervent prayer at the Temple, Hezekiah petitioned the Lord for deliverance (2 Kings 19:14–19). Intercessory prayer was an important aspect of the ministry of the prophets (for example, Exodus 32:31–32; 33:12–17; Numbers 14:13–19; 1 Samuel 7:8–9; 12:19, 23; Jeremiah 15:1). Not only did Hezekiah act as the prophets did but he acted in the similitude of Jesus Christ, whose final, great intercessory prayer pleaded for the welfare, protection, deliverance, and unity of all his disciples (John 17).

Isaiah responded on behalf of Jehovah with an oracle against Assyria, rich in powerful poetic imagery (2 Kings 19:20–34). Jerusalem could "laugh" Assyria "to scorn," he said, for the invaders had not offended mere mortals; they had "reproached and blasphemed" the Holy One of Israel (2 Kings 19:21–22). Concerning Assyria's king, "he shall not come into this city, nor shoot an arrow there, nor come before it with shield, nor cast a [siege] bank against it. By the way that he came, by the same shall he return, and shall not come into this city, saith the Lord. For I will defend this city, to save it" (2 Kings 19:32–34).

Through divine intervention, Sennacherib did abandon his planned attack on Jerusalem. At night an "angel of the Lord went out, and smote in the camp of the Assyrians a hundred fourscore and five thousand; and when they who were left arose early in the morning" they found the bodies of those who were smitten (JST 2 Kings 19:35). Some scholars have proposed that an epidemic struck the Assyrian troops. Others postulate that rumors of revolt back home forced Sennacherib to pull out. Whatever method the Lord used, the Assyrian demise was an act of God, in clear fulfillment of prophetic promises. It is imperative that its message not be obscured: the Lord delivers his righteous people "out of the hand of all [their] enemies" (2 Kings 17:39). Hezekiah was a partner in this deliverance and acted in similitude of the Heavenly King of deliverance—constant, encouraging, and positive. "Thus the Lord saved Hezekiah and the inhabitants of Jerusalem from the hand of Sennacherib the king of Assyria, and from the hand of all other, and guided them on every side. And many brought gifts unto the Lord to Jerusalem, and presents to Hezekiah king of Judah: so that he was magnified in the sight of all nations from thenceforth" (2 Chronicles 32:22–23).

Sennacherib's death also occurred as Isaiah had predicted (2 Kings 19:7, 36–37). He was assassinated in 681 B.C. as a result of some palace intrigue, and his son Esarhaddon (680–669) B.C.) came to the throne, followed by Ashurbanipal (668–627 B.C). After that, Assyria's power was soon eclipsed by that of Babylon, who ultimately destroyed Jerusalem and the Temple and carried away Judah into captivity.

The record of Hezekiah in 2 Kings includes an episode in which the king learned by revelation of his own imminent death (2 Kings 20:1–11). With faith Hezekiah asked the Lord to grant him continued life and was promised fifteen more years. "I have heard thy prayer," the Lord said, and "I will heal thee" (2 Kings 20:5). Hezekiah was also granted a sign that he would be blessed.

Even though Hezekiah was a similitude of the coming King-Messiah, he was still mortal and made mistakes. The authors of Kings and Chronicles candidly recorded some things he did wrong (2 Chronicles 32:25–26). He made a big mistake when he showed his kingdom's wealth to the messengers of Babylon, for in due time, as Isaiah pointed out to him, the Babylonians would return to take possession of it (2 Kings 20:12–18; 2 Chronicles 32:31).

But even with weaknesses, Hezekiah clearly was one of the greatest—perhaps *the* greatest, as the sacred historian suggested (2 Kings 18:5)—of all the kings who ever presided over Israel and Judah, including David and Solomon. He was great because he trusted in the Lord and governed his kingdom in harmony with divine will, following the guidance of the prophet whom the Lord sent to assist him. Here was a king on the throne of his father David who exemplified righteous kingship. In that way, he foreshadowed the greatest of all rulers, his future descendant Jesus Christ, who one day would come as King of kings.

CHAPTER 12

ISAIAH AND JEREMIAH
SIMILITUDES DURING
IMPENDING DOOM

Isaiah and Jeremiah are two of the most important, well-known, and often-quoted prophets in Israelite history. They demonstrated characteristics in common with each other and with Jesus of Nazareth that show them to be profound similitudes of our Lord. They also possessed characteristics and engaged in actions different from each other but which also pointed to the life of the Messiah and paralleled it.

Like Jesus, both Isaiah and Jeremiah ministered in times of political upheaval and threat from the great empires of their day. For Isaiah it was the Assyrians, for Jeremiah it was the Babylonians, and for Jesus it was the Romans. Like Jesus, both prophets had to preach in the face of rampant apostasy. All three called for a complete reformation of society. And like Jesus, both Isaiah and Jeremiah were killed for the sake of the truth and the kingdom of God. According to tradition, Isaiah was "sawn asunder," and Jeremiah was stoned to death.[1] Both prophets, "like most of the Lord's anointed in ancient times, . . . sealed [their] mission and [their] works with [their] own blood" (D&C 135:3).

Isaiah's ministry overlapped the reigns of four kings of

Judah—Uzziah, Jotham, Ahaz, and Hezekiah—and lasted from approximately 742 to 700 B.C. His call to be a prophet came as he saw the Lord while in the Temple and exemplifies the nature of a similitude. Even though the presence of the Lord caused Isaiah to feel "undone," unworthy, and unclean (Isaiah 6:5), he responded *exactly* as the Savior had responded long before in the premortal council. "Also I heard the voice of the Lord, saying, Whom shall I send, and who will go for us? Then said I, Here am I; send me" (Isaiah 6:8; compare Abraham 3:27). This impressive parallel between Isaiah and Jesus Christ portended the close association the prophet would have with the Lord during his mortal life.

More of Isaiah's words became the Savior's words than those of any other prophet. That is, Jesus quoted Isaiah more frequently than he quoted any other prophet. He told us why after he was resurrected, and in so doing gave to the Nephites a unique endorsement of Isaiah: "And now, behold, I say unto you, that ye ought to search these things. Yea, a commandment I give unto you that ye search these things diligently; for great are the words of Isaiah. For surely he spake as touching all things concerning my people which are of the house of Israel; therefore it must needs be that he must speak also to the Gentiles. And all things that he spake have been and shall be, even according to the words which he spake" (3 Nephi 23:1–3).

Isaiah had panoramic visions and apparently saw more, or at least was told to present more, of Jesus' life and ministry than any of the other prophets. Undoubtedly Jehovah foreknew that he would not only quote Isaiah's words but speak them as though they were his very own during his mortal ministry. When Jesus quoted Isaiah's words, they became an unmistakable declaration of his messianic calling. This was the case early in his ministry when he spoke to the people in his hometown on the Sabbath and quoted Isaiah 61:1–2:

"And he came to Nazareth, where he had been brought up: and as his custom was, he went into the synagogue on the sabbath day, and stood up for to read.

"And there was delivered unto him the book of the prophet Esaias. And when he had opened the book, he found the place where it was written,

"The Spirit of the Lord is upon me, because he hath anointed me to preach the gospel to the poor; he hath sent me to heal the broken-hearted, to preach deliverance to the captives, and recovering of sight to the blind, to set at liberty them that are bruised,

"To preach the acceptable year of the Lord.

"And he closed the book, and he gave it again to the minister, and sat down. And the eyes of all them that were in the synagogue were fastened on him.

"And he began to say unto them. This day is this scripture fulfilled in your ears.

"And all bare him witness and wondered at the gracious words which proceeded out of his mouth. And they said, Is not this Joseph's son?" (Luke 4:16–22).

Like Jesus, the prophet-poet Isaiah used metaphor heavily to describe the condition of the proud people of Israel and their spiritual needs. For example, during his call, Isaiah was told, "Make the heart of this people fat, and make their ears heavy, and shut their eyes; lest they see with their eyes, and hear with their ears, and understand with their heart, and convert, and be healed" (Isaiah 6:10). Centuries later, Jesus used this very passage in explaining why he spoke in parables after he had just given the parable of the sower to a great multitude (Matthew

13:13–16; Mark 4:12; Luke 8:10). In so doing, he was telling the people that he identified with Isaiah and that that prophet's setting and circumstances were his own setting and circumstances. Again, just as Isaiah pointed to Jesus, Jesus pointed back to Isaiah.

One of the most unusual types or similitudes of Christ in the Old Testament is associated with the birth of one of Isaiah's sons. King Rezin of Syria and King Pekah of the northern kingdom of Israel tried to persuade King Ahaz of the southern kingdom of Judah to ally with them against Assyria. Isaiah, however, tried to persuade Ahaz to trust in the Lord for deliverance from the invading army (Isaiah 7:1–9). Isaiah even offered to provide a sign to persuade Ahaz and to demonstrate that events would unfold as Isaiah prophesied. Ahaz rejected the opportunity to have a sign, but the Lord provided one anyway. The sign had to do with a specific virgin who would conceive, bring forth a son, and call his name Immanuel:

"Moreover the Lord spake again unto Ahaz, saying, Ask thee a sign of the Lord thy God; ask it either in the depth, or in the height above. But Ahaz said, I will not ask, neither will I tempt the Lord. And he said, Hear ye now, O house of David; Is it a small thing for you to weary men, but will ye weary my God also? Therefore the Lord himself shall give you a sign; Behold, a virgin shall conceive, and bear a son and shall call his name Immanuel. Butter and honey shall he eat, that he may know to refuse the evil, and choose the good. For before the child shall know to refuse the evil, and choose the good, the land that thou abhorrest shall be forsaken of both her kings" (Isaiah 7:10–16).

It has been noted that "the prophecy has a dual application, as shown by a close reading of Isaiah 7:10–16; 8:3–7; and

Matthew 1:21. First, the greater fulfillment of the prophecy centers in Jesus Christ, who was Immanuel, the son of the virgin Mary. Matthew recorded this fulfillment: 'She shall bring forth a son, and thou shalt call his name Jesus: for he shall save his people from their sins. Now all this was done, that it might be fulfilled which was spoken of the Lord by the prophet [Isaiah], saying, Behold, a virgin shall be with child, and shall bring forth a son, and they shall call his name Emmanuel, which being interpreted is, God with us' (Matthew 1:21–23). Second, because the sign was given, in part, to nurture Ahaz's faith, it would have had some fulfillment in his lifetime. The lesser fulfillment of the Immanuel prophecy thus pertains to Isaiah's wife, the prophetess, who also fulfilled the conditions of Isaiah's prophecy when she brought forth a son. Isaiah, the prophetess, their son, and the conditions surrounding his birth all point to the birth of Jesus Christ."[2]

Isaiah's language in Isaiah 8:3–7 shows that the first fulfillment of the so-called "Immanuel prophecy" in Isaiah 7:10–16 was connected to himself, his wife, and their son:

"And I went unto the prophetess; and she conceived, and bare a son. Then said the Lord to me, Call his name Maher-shalal-hash-baz. For before the child shall have knowledge to cry, My father, and my mother, the riches of Damascus and the spoil of Samaria shall be taken away before the king of Assyria. The Lord spake also unto me again, saying, Forasmuch as this people refuseth the waters of Shiloah that go softly and rejoice in Rezin and Remaliah's son; Now therefore, behold, the Lord bringeth up upon them the waters of the river, strong and many, even the king of Assyria, and all his glory: and he shall come up over all his channels, and go over all his banks" (Isaiah 8:3–7).

Matthew's language in Matthew 1:21–23 shows that the second and greater fulfillment of Isaiah's prophecy in the meridian of time pertained to Jesus: "And she shall bring forth a son, and thou shalt call his name JESUS: for he shall save his people from their sins. Now all this was done, that it might be fulfilled which was spoken of the Lord by the prophet, saying, Behold a virgin shall be with child, and shall bring forth a son, and they shall call his name Emmanuel, which being interpreted is, God with us" (Matthew 1:21–23).

The name of Isaiah's son who first fulfilled the "Immanuel prophecy" is Maher-shalal-hash-baz (children today should never complain about their names!). The name means, literally, "to speed, spoil, hasten, plunder." Out of the name comes the lesson. "Maher-shalal-hash-baz is a type of Jesus Christ. Both Maher-shalal-hash-baz and Christ possess prophetic names; the name *Maher-shalal-hash-baz* has four parts, similar to the four titles of Jesus found in Isaiah 9:6. Both were named by revelation from God, and both entered the world during times of political upheaval and warfare. *Maher-shalal-hash-baz* prophesies the manner in which Israel would be speedily destroyed and then plundered; likewise, Jesus Christ will come down to judge the world and speedily destroy those who are wicked. Jewish tradition holds that the prophetess belonged to a royal line. If this is indeed true, then Maher-shalal-hash-baz was of royal lineage, as was Jesus Christ."[3]

Other scholars translate Maher-shalal-hash-baz more freely, "Destruction is coming quickly," and thus make the similitude easier to discern. Christ is coming quickly, and his coming shall be a day of destruction for the wicked. As for Isaiah's other son, She'ar Yashuv, they see another similitude of Christ. The name means "a remnant shall return" and points to Christ in that the righteous remnant of the Lord's people shall be spared and exalted at Christ's coming.[4]

No matter how one views the specifics, the point is well established: Isaiah understood the nature of types and similitudes and so honored his sons by linking them to the Messiah and to Israelite history through their names. These sons were a constant reminder to Isaiah's countrymen. But, then again, so was Isaiah himself: his name means "The Lord is salvation" or "Jehovah saves."

Even more than being a type and similitude of Jesus Christ, Isaiah was a revealer of the Savior's first and second comings. These prophecies are so many and so profound that they require a separate study. But some of the more significant of these revelations about the Savior's mortal life are helpful in rounding out our discussion of Isaiah and in validating, at a glance, the declaration of the Savior, "Great are the words of Isaiah" (3 Nephi 23:1). Many of these verses are so filled with feeling that it is as though Isaiah had experienced for himself the very situations and circumstances that he described. Such is the nature of a revelator who was also a similitude.

ISAIAH PASSAGE	DESCRIPTION OF JESUS' LIFE AND MINISTRY
7:14; 9:6–7	Born of a virgin; roles; lineage
11:1, 10; 53:1–3; 60:6	Lineage; personality, example, the Magi
6:9–10; 8:14	Teachings rejected; an offense to Israel
9:1; 28:16	Place of ministry, cornerstone of the plan
40:3, 9–11; 42:1–5	Work of a forerunner and his message
49:7–8; 52:3, 4–15	Redeems though despised; a helper, a restorer
50:6–7	Scourged and smitten but determined
53:4–12; 61:1–2; 63:3	Suffering, Atonement, death, deliverance to captives
22:22–25	Crucifixion

Though Isaiah was a prophet for the kingdom of Judah, his message is for all humankind. Though he lived seven centuries before the earthly Messiah, he knew the Lord Jesus Christ personally and knew his life in detailed ways.

JEREMIAH

Jeremiah was born of a priestly family in the village of Anathoth, about three miles northeast of Jerusalem (Jeremiah 1:1). Thus, Jeremiah was a prophet and priest in Israel. He received his call in 627 B.C. and ministered forty years, until 587 B.C., the year of the destruction of Jerusalem and the Temple.

Jeremiah's call was introduced by an extraordinary and famous revelation in which the Lord described Jeremiah's premortal preparation: "Before I formed thee in the belly I knew thee; and before thou camest forth out of the womb I sanctified thee, and I ordained thee a prophet unto the nations" (Jeremiah 1:5). Jeremiah was a type and similitude of Jesus Christ who, we are told, was sanctified and foreordained and prepared from the foundation of the world (1 Peter 1:20; Revelation 13:8; Ether 3:14). Of the Savior's foreordained preparation, the Prophet Joseph Smith said, "At the first organization in heaven we were all present, and saw the Savior chosen and appointed and the plan of salvation made, and we sanctioned it."[5]

As a similitude of Christ, Jeremiah faced the same kind of opposition, insults, and attempts on his life as Jesus did—all from members of the house of Israel. This parallels the sobering warning found in the Book of Mormon. The greatest persecutors of the Lord and his special witnesses are, shockingly, members of the house of Israel: "And the multitude of the earth was gathered together; and I beheld that they were in a large and spacious building, like unto the building which my father saw. And the angel of the Lord spake unto me again, saying: Behold the world and the wisdom thereof; yea, behold the house of Israel hath gathered together to fight against the twelve apostles of the Lamb" (1 Nephi 11:35).

Jeremiah said that because the Lord revealed to him the evil intents and doings of the house of Israel and the house of Judah, he knew he was in for trouble: "But I was like a lamb or an ox that is brought to the slaughter; and I knew not that they had devised devices against me, saying, Let us destroy the tree with the fruit thereof, and let us cut him off from the land of the living, that his name may be no more remembered" (Jeremiah 11:19). In other words, because Jeremiah had no children (Jeremiah 16:2), by killing him, though he was as innocent as a lamb, persecutors thought his name would die with him.

One immediately recognizes that this circumstance articulated in Jeremiah 11:19 also applies to both Jesus Christ (Isaiah quotes it in Isaiah 53:7, when describing the Savior's suffering) and the Prophet Joseph Smith. The latter lamented when he went to Carthage to surrender himself to the pretended requirements of the law that he that was "going like a lamb to the slaughter" (D&C 135:4). Jesus, Jeremiah, and Joseph Smith all faced parallel circumstances surrounding their deaths.

Both Jeremiah and Jesus tried to stem the tide of immorality, feelings of prideful superiority, and misplaced fanatical confidence in God's favoritism. Their single-minded efforts earned them the wrath of their countrymen.

One of the more interesting and important parallels between Jeremiah and Jesus that helps us to see Jeremiah more clearly as a similitude of Jesus centers on the interaction between the two anointed leaders and the priests of the Temple. The following summary may be helpful:[6]

> Both Jeremiah and Jesus preached in the court of the Temple (compare Jeremiah 26:1–2 and Matthew 21:23–23:36).

> Both preached following a divine mandate but with no guarantee of success (compare Jeremiah 26:3–6 and Matthew 21:33–39).

> Both prophesied the destruction of the Temple (compare Jeremiah 26:4–7 and Matthew 24:1–2).

> Priests were involved in arresting both Jeremiah and Jesus and charging them with prophesying falsely (compare Jeremiah 26:8–9 and Matthew 26:47, 59; Mark 14:43, 55–64).

> Both Jeremiah and Jesus received some kind of hearing or arraignment within the Temple precinct under priestly jurisdiction (compare Jeremiah 26:9 and Matthew 26:57; Mark 14:53).

> In the cases of both Jeremiah and Jesus, secular authority convened a court (compare Jeremiah 26:10 and Matthew 27:11; Mark 15:1–2).

> With both, the priests framed the case before secular authority (compare Jeremiah 26:11 and Matthew 27:12, Mark 15:3).

> Both Jeremiah and Jesus defended themselves by referring to divine mandate (compare Jeremiah 26:12 and Matthew 26:64).

> In both cases, the secular ruler declared an intention to

exonerate the accused (compare Jeremiah 26:16 and Matthew 27:23; Luke 23:4, 13–14).

In both cases, a comparison was made with another accused, whose fate was also hanging in the balance (compare Jeremiah 26:20–22 and Matthew 27:15–26).

It is significant that the foregoing parallel between Jeremiah and Jesus comes from Jeremiah 26, which, though an account of Jeremiah's temple sermon, is really a similitude of the Savior's arrest and arraignment. Of course, Jeremiah was not immediately executed and Jesus was. But in the end, Jeremiah was executed as well. And, thus, ultimately Jeremiah's life was a powerful similitude and foreshadowing of the earthly life of the God that Jeremiah served with patience, fortitude, and steadiness.

Like Jesus, Jeremiah lived in turbulent times. Both witnessed a society spiraling downwards. Jeremiah shared a prophetic stewardship with other prophets—Zephaniah, Habakkuk, Nahum, Lehi, and Ezekiel—all of whom, like Jesus six hundred years later, testified that Judah and Jerusalem must repent or perish. Jeremiah, like Jesus, addressed a hard-hearted, stiff-necked people. This message fell on deaf ears, and, as in Jesus' day, destruction followed the unheeded warnings. The Jerusalem Temple was destroyed, and the Jews were scattered by a powerful empire. The events of 587 B.C. were replayed in A.D. 70 with even greater intensity and horror. Jeremiah's life was a pattern of Jesus' life; what happened in Jeremiah's day was repeated in the meridian of time.

CHAPTER 13

CYRUS

A UNIQUE MESSIAH

The destruction of Jerusalem (587 B.C.) and the Babylonian exile (587–538 B.C.) were times of great sorrow for the kingdom of Judah, but the Lord had said that his city and his people would not be forgotten. He would raise up a deliverer to bring down Babylon and cause Jerusalem, along with the holy Temple, to be rebuilt. That deliverer would be an instrument in God's hands, and his name would be Cyrus: "Thus said the Lord, thy redeemer, . . . I am the Lord that maketh all things; . . . that saith to Jerusalem, Thou shalt be inhabited; and to the cities of Judah, Ye shall be built, and I will raise up the decayed places thereof: that saith of Cyrus, He is my shepherd, and shall perform all my pleasure: even saying to Jerusalem, Thou shalt be built; and to the temple, Thy foundation shall be laid" (Isaiah 44:24–28). Though Cyrus, king of Persia, was a Gentile king of the Near East (559–530 B.C.) there is no doubt that he was a type and similitude of the true Messiah who would come more than five hundred years after his pivotal reign.

Cyrus was born into a Persian noble family, the Achaemenids, of unknown date. He emerged in history around 559 B.C. as he began to create an empire that took twenty years to consolidate but which lasted two hundred years. In 539 B.C. Cyrus moved against the Babylonian Empire and took control of it, including the community of Israelites that had been exiled by the Babylonians when they destroyed Jerusalem and the Temple. Cyrus's historical record, the Cyrus Cylinder (made of clay), makes it clear that the great king was seen as a liberator. Cyrus claimed to follow an enlightened policy toward conquered or subjugated peoples. Cyrus said he abolished forced labor, improved housing conditions, and enjoyed the affection of the populace as a benevolent despot.

Though written as propaganda for his time, such a favorable view is not unjustified. Cyrus seems to have understood the futility of trying to compel loyalty through violence and terror. He also stated that he "did not allow anybody to terrorize [any place]."[1] Compared with other conquerors of ancient times, especially the Assyrians and Babylonians, Cyrus was extraordinarily humane, even benevolent at times. Perhaps this was so because God had chosen him as an instrument to help bring about divine purposes.

In the only Old Testament passage where the term "messiah" or "anointed one" is used to refer to a non-Israelite, the relationship between the Lord and Cyrus is outlined. The passage is Isaiah 45:1–3, and it attributes Cyrus's success to Jehovah's divine design:

"Thus saith the Lord to his anointed, to Cyrus, whose right hand I have holden, to subdue nations before him; and I will loose the loins of kings, to open before him the two leaved gates; and the gates shall not be shut;

"I will go before thee, and make the crooked places straight:

I will break in pieces the gates of brass, and cut in sunder the bars of iron:

"And I will give thee the treasures of darkness, and hidden riches of secret places, that thou mayest know that I, the Lord, which call thee by thy name, am the God of Israel" (Isaiah 45:1–3).

The Lord went on to say that he had called Cyrus by his name and had given Cyrus his honorary title (the Hebrew word *kan'ak* can mean either "surname" or "honorary title") for the sake of Israel. "For Jacob my servant's sake, and Israel mine elect, I have even called thee by thy name: I have surnamed [*Kan'ak*] thee, though thou hast not known me" (Isaiah 45:4). Cyrus was given victory, honor, and kingship not for his personal benefit but so that Israel could be blessed and, in turn, bless others.

This is an important principle for modern disciples to learn. We are called and blessed in order to bless others. The Prophet Joseph Smith used this very passage, Isaiah 45:4, to teach this principle: "That we may learn still further that God calls or elects particular men to perform particular works, or on whom to confer special blessings, we read, . . . 'For Jacob my servant's sake, and Israel mine elect, I have even called thee [Cyrus] by thy name,' to be a deliverer to my people Israel, and help to plant them on my holy mountain."[2]

Writing in the first century after Christ, the Jewish historian Josephus indicated that Isaiah's prophecies themselves had a great effect on Cyrus once he entered Babylon and was shown the sacred writings of the Israelite exiles. In fact, Josephus portrayed the comments of Cyrus as a response motivated by the Lord's declarations in scripture:

"For he [the Lord] stirred up the mind of Cyrus and made him write this throughout all Asia:—'Thus saith Cyrus the

King:—Since God Almighty hath appointed me to be king of the habitable earth, I believe that he is that God which the nation of the Israelites worship; for indeed he foretold my name by the prophets, and that I should build him a house at Jerusalem, in the country of Judea.' This was known to Cyrus by his reading the book which Isaiah left behind him of his prophecies; for this prophet said that God had spoken thus to him in a secret vision: 'My will is, that Cyrus, whom I have appointed to be king over many and great nations, send back my people to their own land, and build my temple.' This was foretold by Isaiah one hundred and forty years before the temple was demolished. Accordingly, when Cyrus read this, and admired the Divine power, an earnest desire and ambition seized upon him to fulfill what was so written."[3]

Although it is not known who was responsible for pointing out to Cyrus the Old Testament prophecies concerning himself, it is possible that one of the prophets of the Exile, such as Daniel, tutored the Persian emperor. More important, however, is the truth that Cyrus was a type and shadow of the Messiah. Cyrus was a deliverer and an instrument in the hands of God to bring about Israel's temporal redemption. Cyrus was designated a "messiah" by the Lord himself. Cyrus permitted the inhabitants of the kingdom of Judah to return to the promised land, and he ordered the Jerusalem Temple to be rebuilt with money from his own treasury. Further, he ordered that the vessels and accoutrements that Nebuchadnezzar had taken from the Temple be returned. All of this made possible the restoration of the sacrificial system, the ordinances which heralded the great and last sacrifice of the Lamb of God.

It is against the foregoing historical and theological background that the opening verses of the book of Ezra are to be understood. In Cyrus's first year as king of Babylon (538 B.C.), the Lord indeed "stirred up the spirit of Cyrus king of Persia, that he made a proclamation" (Ezra 1:1), a proclamation which has come to be known as the Edict of Liberation. The edict is preserved in the book of Ezra in two versions. One (Ezra 1:2–4) is written in Hebrew, the traditional biblical language of Israel and Judah. The other (Ezra 6:3–5) is written in Aramaic, the diplomatic language of the Persian Empire, which gradually became the common tongue of the Jewish people during the post-Exilic period.[4]

HEBREW VERSION

Thus saith Cyrus king of Persia, The Lord God of heaven hath given me all the kingdoms of the earth; and he hath charged me to build him an house at Jerusalem, which is in Judah. Who is there among you of all his people? his God be with him, and let him go up to Jerusalem, which is in Judah, and build the house of the Lord God of Israel, (he is the God,) which is in Jerusalem. And whosoever remaineth in any place where he sojourneth, let the men of his place help him with silver, and with gold, and with goods, and with beasts, beside the freewill offering for the house of God that is in Jerusalem. (Ezra 1:2–4)

ARAMAIC VERSION

In the first year of Cyrus the king[,] the same Cyrus the king made a decree concerning the house of God at Jeusalem, Let the house be builded, the place where they offered sacrifices, and let the foundations thereof be strongly laid; the height thereof threescore cubits, and the breadth thereof threescore cubits; with three rows of great stones, and a row of new timber: and let the expenses be given out of the king's house: and also let the golden and silver vessels of the house of God, which Nebuchadnezzar took forth out of the temple which is at Jerusalem, and brought unto Babylon, be restored, and brought again unto the temple which is at Jerusalem, every one to his place, and place them in the house of God. (Ezra 6:3 5)

Although there has been some discussion about which version of the edict represents the original document and which is a translation, the historicity of Cyrus's decree is beyond doubt. The very fact that the edict is preserved in two versions speaks for its authenticity. It is probable that the Hebrew text (Ezra 1:2–4) represents the oral proclamation of the decree and the Aramaic text (Ezra 6:3–5) the official written decree. The edict is also substantiated by an independent source, the Cyrus Cylinder itself. In one passage of the cylinder, Cyrus declared: "I returned to (these) sacred cities on the other side of the Tigris, the sanctuaries of which have been ruins for a long time, the images which (used) to live therein and established for them permanent sanctuaries. I (also) gathered all their (former) inhabitants and returned (to them) their habitations."[5]

In the April 1972 general conference, then-Elder Ezra Taft Benson provided significant insight and commentary about Cyrus's role in our Father's divine plan, as well as the way in which all humanity are used by God to further his divine purposes. Elder Benson had just returned from Iran, in the Middle East, where he had represented the Church at a celebration commemorating the twenty-five-hundredth anniversary of the founding of the Persian Empire by Cyrus the Great. Elder Benson said this:

"Parley P. Pratt, in describing the Prophet Joseph Smith, said that he had 'the boldness, courage, temperance, perseverance and generosity of a Cyrus.' (*Autobiography of Parley Parker Pratt* [Deseret Book Company, 1938], p. 46.)

"President Wilford Woodruff said: 'Now I have thought many times that some of those ancient kings that were raised up, had in some respects more regard for carrying out of some of these principles and laws, than even the Latter-day Saints have in our day. I will take as an ensample Cyrus . . . To trace the life of Cyrus from his birth to his death, whether he knew it or not, it looked as though he lived by inspiration in all his movements.' . . .

"God, the Father of us all, uses the men of the earth, especially good men, to accomplish his purposes. It has been true in the past, it is true today, it will be true in the future.

" 'Perhaps the Lord needs such men on the outside of His Church to help it along,' said the late Elder Orson F. Whitney of the Quorum of the Twelve. 'They are among its auxiliaries, and can do more good for the cause where the Lord has placed them, than anywhere else. . . . Hence, some are drawn into the fold and receive a testimony of the truth; while others remain unconverted . . . the beauties and glories of the gospel being veiled temporarily from their view, for a wise purpose. The Lord will open their eyes in His own due time. God is using more than one people for the accomplishment of His great and marvelous work. The Latter-day Saints cannot do it all. It is too vast, too arduous for any one people. . . . We have no quarrel with the Gentiles. They are our partners in a certain sense' (*Conference Report,* April 1928, p. 59.)."[6]

Elder Benson's statement is remarkable and worthy of our repeated study. It was prompted by his understanding of the important place of Cyrus in the Lord's plan. From one of the Lord's special witnesses and a future Church president, we are given a declaration of the greatness of both Cyrus and Joseph Smith. Cyrus was the anointed of Jehovah. In fact, Cyrus parallels the latter-day Prophet of the Restoration as well as the Lord Jesus Christ in that he delivered the captives of Israel, restored the kingdom of Judah to independent status so that they could worship the true and living God, and laid the foundation for the reconstruction of the house of the Lord—the most important place on earth in any dispensation.

From Elder Benson we receive a sure witness that God has a plan and He controls its fulfillment. He has a timetable for all of his children. The Lord uses *all* men to accomplish his purposes but especially good men. All things are in his hands. We also learn that the Lord is behind the timetable of the conversion process of those whose hearts are pure, who possess a disposition of faith, and who seek for and honor the truth, no matter the circumstances in which they find themselves.

The great lesson for students of the Old Testament is that the ancient record is filled with similitudes and foreshadowings—of Jesus Christ, of Joseph Smith, of modern prophets, and of timeless standards of behavior. If, as Elder Benson testifies, the Lord actually veils the beauties of the gospel from the view of some of his children for his own purposes, we must take seriously the observation that we are not in charge and we do not convert people to the truth—the Lord does! It is incumbent upon us to be more tolerant of others, to appreciate more the goodness of those who are not members of our Church. We must become more patient and kind, less bellicose and less upset when others reject our message. Perhaps it is part of God's design. We must continue to preach the gospel with all our might but be less judgmental and more Christlike.

The great meaning of Cyrus's designation as a messiah is that the Lord works outside the parameters of natural, mortal, fallen man's thinking and presuppositions. There are many similitudes of Christ and some of them may even surround us.

CHAPTER 14

ESTHER, DEBORAH, AND HULDAH

WOMEN OF POWER AND MESSIANIC PORTENT

During the Babylonian captivity of the kingdom of Judah (587–538 B.C.), things looked bleak for the covenant people. Their temple was gone; their capital city lay in ruins; their God had seemed to abandon them. But after the Babylonians were overthrown by the Persians under the leadership of Cyrus the Great, the imperial centers where the deported peoples were living became acceptable, even desirable, places for the Jews to reside—so much so that when the captives were free to return to their homeland, a great number of them chose to remain in the Persian east, under direct control of the Persian king. After a time, however, during the reign of King Ahasuerus, known in historical records as Xerxes (486–465 B.C.), a crisis of gargantuan proportions threatened to destroy the Jewish people. The story is recorded in the book of Esther, whose heroine not only gave the text its name but also delivered her people in a way that also foreshadowed and paralleled, on a lesser scale, the future deliverance provided by Jesus of Nazareth.

King Ahasuerus had made a feast for the princes and nobles of his realm, the powerbrokers of the empire. He commanded his personal attendants to bring Queen Vashti before the royal court in order to show off her tremendous beauty. She refused to be coerced. The king's anger burned hot. He deposed Vashti and sought a new queen because of her perceived insolence and challenge to his authority, his own embarrassment, and the fear that an outbreak of disobedience by the wives of other leaders might follow (Esther 1:10–18).

The reasons or motives for Vashti's disobedience to the king are not disclosed in the scriptures. It is more than possible, however, that Vashti, though not an Israelite, is also a true hero of the Old Testament. Her refusal to be paraded in front of the royal court may well have been based on a profound sense of propriety, a desire to uphold the principles of modesty, virtue, and dignity. After all, King Ahasuerus had made his regrettable request only after he and his guests had been drinking for seven days and were "merry with wine" (Esther 1:10). The later rabbis taught that the king demanded Vashti appear before the royal court naked.[1]

The first-century Jewish historian Josephus attributed noble motives to Vashti: "Now the king was desirous to shew her, who exceeded all other women in beauty, to those that feasted with him, and he sent some to command her to come to his feast. But she, out of regard to the laws of the Persians, which forbid the wives to be seen by strangers, did not go to the king; and though he oftentimes sent the eunuchs to her, she did nevertheless stay away, and refused to come, till the king was so much irritated."[2]

Josephus further indicated that after King Ahasuerus sobered up, he realized the mistake he had made in issuing an irrevocable edict to replace his beloved queen. "But the king having been fond of her, he did not well bear a separation, and yet by the law he could not admit of a reconciliation, so he was under trouble, as not having it in his power to do what he desired to do: but when his friends saw him so uneasy, they advised him to cast the memory of his wife, and his love for her, out of his mind, but to send abroad . . . and to search out for comely virgins, and to take her whom he should best like for his wife."[3] Josephus's account corroborates the part of the biblical text which indicates that when the anger of the king subsided, he remembered with regret what had transpired (Esther 2:1).

Based on the evidence presented by Josephus, Vashti's example is one of Christlike behavior in the face of grave consequences. Even though she was not a member of the covenant community, she serves as a model for both men and women of all generations. When power is invoked in haste, or used to coerce, or sets at naught the prized principle of virtue, or diminishes individual dignity, sadness is the ultimate result. Those who pay a price to uphold standards of propriety are to be honored.

ESTHER

After a kingdom-wide search, Esther was chosen as queen to replace Vashti. Her beauty was unsurpassed, and she won the favor of everyone, including King Ahasuerus (Esther 2:2–18). But Esther had a secret. She had not told anyone in the government that she was Jewish and the adopted daughter of Mordecai, an older cousin who had raised her after her parents died (Esther 2:20).

This secret set the stage for the coming crisis, for against righteous Esther and Mordecai was Haman, one of the nobles of the realm who had been elevated by the king to the position of chief minister (Esther 3:1). All who passed by Haman bowed to him and did obeisance because of his high position—all except for Mordecai. He refused because, as he said, he was a Jew (Esther 3:2–4). Such deference to government leaders was not forbidden by Jewish law, but nonbiblical texts supply a detail omitted in the biblical record: "Haman claimed divine honors for himself."[4] From this point on, Haman was filled with wrath and "sought to destroy all the Jews that were throughout the whole kingdom of Ahasuerus, even the people of Mordecai" (Esther 3:6).

For several months, lots (dice) were cast until the most propitious day was found on which Haman could propose to the king a pogrom, or systematic destruction of the Jews. Haman pointed out to the king that the Jews were different from the other peoples of the realm, that they did not keep the king's laws, and that it would be in the king's best interest to have them destroyed. He even offered to pay ten thousand talents of silver into the royal treasury to offset the cost of the dreadful work of death. But the king told him to keep his money and do with the Jewish people as he pleased. Haman therefore had an official decree drawn up and issued to the provincial governors to "destroy, to kill, and to cause to perish, all Jews, both young and old, little children and women, in one day," and take the spoils of the people (Esther 3:13). Then "the king and Haman sat down to drink; but the city Shushan was perplexed" (Esther 3:15), meaning that the capital city was thrown into consternation over the ominous decree. These were dark days indeed.

When Mordecai learned all that had been done, he tore his clothing, put on sackcloth and ashes, and mourned with the Jews. More important, Mordecai sent a request to Queen

Esther, asking her to go to the king and make supplication on behalf of the Jewish people, entreating him to reverse the decree of destruction. Esther responded by reminding Mordecai that, by law, anyone who appeared before the king without invitation could be put to death—and she had not been called to attend the king for thirty days. Mordecai wisely counseled Esther that just because she was in the palace did not mean she would escape the fate of all the other Jews of the realm (Esther 4:4–13). In fact, if she kept silent, said Mordecai, relief and deliverance would surely arise from another quarter. But just maybe, by refusing to act, Esther would be missing out on her foreordained mission. Perhaps Esther herself had been raised up by God for precisely that very moment for the specific purpose of bringing deliverance to an entire nation.

In that comment is the great lesson that applies to each one of us at our particular moment in the history of the kingdom of God. Each of us must seriously consider Mordecai's question: "And who knoweth whether thou art come to the kingdom for such a time as this?" (Esther 4:14).

Esther answered Mordecai in true heroic fashion, in a way that bespoke the great spiritual maturity, power, and faith that were hers and that are her legacy: "Go, gather together all the Jews that are present in Shushan, and fast ye for me, and neither eat nor drink three days, night or day: I also and my maidens will fast likewise; and so will I go in unto the king, which is not according to the law: and if I perish, I perish" (Esther 4:16).

Her statement reflects the same ultimate commitment to follow God's will that Jesus possessed and uttered in his gravest hour of peril and challenge (see Matthew 26:39; Mark 14:36; Luke 22:42; D&C 19:18–19). Her response foreshadowed and prefigured the Savior's attitude and actions by several hundred years.

The rest of Esther's story is well known. She was given an audience with the king, who promised to grant her request even "to the half of the kingdom" (Esther 5:3). Ultimately, her request for overturning the decree of destruction was granted, and a new decree was issued. Haman's roles and fortunes were reversed with Mordecai's. In fact, Haman was hanged on the very gallows he had constructed for Mordecai.

"And [Esther] said, If it please the king, and if I have found favour in his sight, and the thing seem right before the king, and I be pleasing in his eyes, let it be written to reverse the letters devised by Haman the son of Hammedatha the Agagite, which he wrote to destroy the Jews which are in all the king's provinces. . . .

"Then the king Ahasuerus said unto Esther the queen and to Mordecai the Jew, Behold, I have given Esther the house of Haman, and him they have hanged upon the gallows, because he laid his hand upon the Jews. . . .

" . . . the king granted the Jews which were in every city to gather themselves together, and to stand for their life, to destroy, to slay, and to cause to perish, all the power of the people and province that would assault them, both little ones and women, and to take the spoil of them for a prey" (Esther 8:5–11).

Because of Esther, an entire people were delivered from destruction. Because of Esther, mercy was instituted and justice accomplished. Because of Esther, the despised became the honored. Because of Esther, the last became the first and the first became the last. Because of Esther, the will of God was accomplished. In all of these things, Esther acted as the anointed of the Lord and acted as the Anointed One acted almost five hundred years later. Esther's accomplishment mirrored the effects of the Atonement, whose saving and redeeming consequences are both temporal and eternal. What has been said of Esther is, in reality, the most significant truth about Jesus: "Esther's elevation became the only hope for an imperiled people."[5] Indeed, Jesus Christ is our only hope and our only deliverance.

Esther is still honored today. The deliverance of the Jewish people resulting from Esther's saving actions is celebrated every year during the festival of Purim. According to the Bible, this holiday derives its name from the non-Hebrew word for the "lots" (*purim*) that were cast by Haman to determine the destruction of the Jewish people (Esther 9:24–27). More than that, Esther's Hebrew name, Hadassah (Esther 2:7), has been given to Jewish relief agencies and hospitals around the world.

DEBORAH

Other powerful women served in ways that paralleled the anointed roles of prophet, priest, and king and foreshadowed the life of the coming Messiah. These women include Deborah, judge and prophetess, and Huldah, prophetess to the people of King Josiah's day (640–609 B.C.). Like Esther, these women not only mirrored the anointed roles held by men in Israelite society but also acted in ways to help deliver, redeem, and guide Israel. In so doing, they foreshadowed the great redemptive act performed by Jesus of Nazareth. These women-deliverers pointed to Christ by carrying out their appointed roles in the manner Jesus carried out his.

Deborah (Hebrew, "bee") served Israel at a challenging time. In fact, the entire two-hundred-year period of the judges, when thirteen individuals gave laws and ministered to Israel, was a time of great wickedness. "In those days . . . every man did that which was right in his own eyes" (Judges 21:25). As a result, the Lord often withdrew his support from his people until they were humbled and turned back to him. He then provided salvation through judges who led Israel. Deborah became a judge at such a time. "And the children of Israel again did evil in the sight of the Lord, when [Judge] Ehud was dead. And the Lord sold [delivered] them into the hand of Jabin king of Canaan. . . . And the children of Israel cried unto the Lord" (Judges 4:1–3). The Lord then raised up Deborah, whom the Bible calls "a prophetess, the wife of Lapidoth, she judged Israel at that time" (Judges 4:4).

Deborah was a person of tremendous emotional and spiritual strength, great wisdom, and prophetic insight. The children of Israel went to her for judgment and guidance (Judges 4:5). To help Israel get out from under the twenty-year oppression of King Jabin and his military commander, Sisera (who had nine hundred iron chariots under his command), Deborah sent for Barak and delivered to him the word of the Lord: "Hath not the Lord God of Israel commanded, saying, Go and draw toward mount Tabor, and take with thee ten thousand men of the children of Naphtali and of the children of Zebulun? And I will draw unto thee to the river Kishon Sisera, the captain of Jabin's army, with his chariots and his multitude; and I will deliver him into thine hand" (Judges 4:6–7).

The Lord, through his prophetess, was telling Israel that he would help them but that they needed to exhibit the faith to follow his instruction—even though his proposed military engagement might have looked risky. Barak was not of the same caliber as Deborah. He said he would follow the counsel of the Lord only if Deborah would go with him. Displaying a kind of courage, faith in God, and leadership that engenders confidence in the leader as well as in God, Deborah said she would go, but she scolded Barak for his lack of courage by telling him, in effect, that because of the way he was going about this, the honor of victory would not be his, for the Lord would hand over Sisera to a woman (Judges 4:9).

Deborah's instruction proved to be inspired. The battle went to Israel. At one point, Deborah further encouraged Barak to exercise full faith by taking advantage of the Lord's help: "And Deborah said unto Barak, Up; for this is the day in which the Lord hath delivered Sisera into thine hand: is not the Lord gone out before thee?" (Judges 4:14). Indeed, with the Lord's help and Deborah's leadership, Israel prevailed so that "there was not a man left" of the enemy (Judges 4:16). As prophesied by Deborah, Sisera was killed by Jael, wife of Heber the Kenite, who had previously had an amicable relationship with Sisera. In one of the most famous stories in the Old Testament, we are told that Jael, by extraordinary cunning, was able to drive a tent spike into Sisera's temple as he slept (see Judges 4:17–22).

Jael herself was a powerful woman of courage as well as mental and emotional toughness. Her actions in taking the life of an opponent of the Lord and his people would be paralleled several hundred years later by Nephi when he slew Laban. When the Spirit commanded Nephi to take Laban's life, Nephi at first questioned the prompting: "Never at any time have I shed the blood of man. And I shrunk and would that I might not slay him. And the Spirit said unto me again: Behold the Lord hath delivered him into thy hands. . . . Behold the Lord slayeth the wicked to bring forth his righteous purposes. It is better that one man should perish than that a nation should dwindle and perish" (1 Nephi 4:10–13). With the help of the

Book of Mormon, it is not hard to understand why Jael did what she did, just as we understand why Nephi did what he did. Difficult, even brutal, times called for men and women of fortitude, who were equal to the distasteful tasks required. Both Deborah and Jael were such women. We who live in modern times ought to be grateful that we do not often have to confront such a brutal environment.

Through Deborah's prophetic leadership, Israel was delivered from great oppression. Deborah's saving ministry points us to Jesus Christ's. He responded perfectly to his foreordained mission; Deborah responded nobly to hers. Jesus delivered the word of God; Deborah delivered the word of God. Jesus did not shrink from his task; Deborah did not shrink from hers. Jesus was a mighty prophet; Deborah a mighty prophetess. Jesus saved his people; Deborah saved hers.

After Israel's victory, Deborah displayed a side of her personality that we often see in great warriors who have had to face much death and destruction—a creative, poetic side (King David is a case in point). Deborah composed and sang a song of victory that praised the Lord's hand in the affairs of humans and highlighted some of the events of the battle. Such poems or songs to commemorate God's involvement in national victories are found throughout early Israelite history (see Exodus 15:1–18; Numbers 21:27–30; Deuteronomy 32:1–43; 1 Samuel 18:7). It is noteworthy that Deborah used phraseology in her song that Paul the apostle later applied to Christ: "Arise, Barak, and lead thy captivity captive" (Judges 5:12). Paul says of the Savior, "When he ascended up on high, he led captivity captive" (Ephesians 4:8). Inspired hymns often point to Christ, as we see in Deborah's case.

It is also stunning that though this powerful prophetess,

judge, and warrior was instrumental in saving a whole nation in time of war, she singled out another role as her most important one in mortality. In her song she exulted, "The inhabitants of the villages ceased, they ceased in Israel, until that I Deborah arose, that I arose a *mother in Israel*" (Judges 5:7; emphasis added). Warriors save nations, but so do mothers. Both are deliverers. The roles of prophet and judge are important and impressive, but for Deborah, these roles grew out of the role that defined who she was fundamentally—a mother in Israel.

HULDAH

A third woman who functioned in a role parallel to the anointed roles of the prophets, priests, and kings of Israel is Huldah. As a prophetess in the days of King Josiah, she is one of the five women designated in the Old Testament as a prophetess. The other four were Miriam, sister of Moses and Aaron (Exodus 15:20); the unnamed wife of the prophet Isaiah (Isaiah 8:3); Noadiah, about whom we know nothing except her name (Nehemiah 6:14); and Deborah (Judges 4–5). In the New Testament period, Anna is called a prophetess. She was at the Jerusalem Temple when the infant Jesus was presented to God by his parents. There Anna identified him as the Messiah and praised God for his arrival (Luke 2:36–38). The four daughters of Philip the evangelist are given special note as those "which did prophesy" (Acts 21:9).

Prophetesses were regarded as possessing special power and special authority. The Lord spoke through them, as Miriam indicated (Numbers 12:1–2). Micah 6:4 speaks of Moses, Aaron, and Miriam as God's special leaders to Israel. Judges 4:6–7 records that Deborah unequivocally delivered the word of the Lord. And 2 Kings is clear that Huldah possessed the power and authority to declare to the people, "Thus saith the Lord God of Israel" (2 Kings 22:15). There is no question that she was revered by the people.

Huldah lived in Jerusalem and offered counsel to the king, the king's counselors, and to the Aaronic priesthood authority who, in her day, was Hilkiah the priest (2 Kings 22:14). She was a blessing to the people and promoted righteousness with her exhortations and her words of comfort. One passage records:

"But to the king of Judah which sent you to enquire of the Lord, thus shall ye say to him, Thus saith the Lord God of Israel, As touching the words which thou hast heard;

"Because thine heart was tender, and thou hast humbled thyself before the Lord, when thou heardest what I spake against this place, and against the inhabitants thereof, that they should become a desolation and a curse, and hast rent thy clothes, and wept before me; I also have heard thee, saith the Lord.

"Behold therefore, I will gather thee unto thy fathers, and thou shalt be gathered into thy grave in peace; and thine eyes shall not see all the evil which I will bring upon this place. And they brought the king word again" (2 Kings 22:18–20).

Josiah was one of the righteous kings of Judah. He worked hard to eradicate the idolatry of past generations and turn his people to the Lord. He restored the Temple to its rightful place of centrality in the kingdom and promoted stricter adherence to the doctrines and practices of the scriptures. At twenty-six years of age, he began repairing the Temple. Workers subsequently discovered an unknown copy of a book of the law—probably a copy of Deuteronomy—and Josiah had it read to him. When he heard how far the Lord's people had strayed from the Lord's commandments and expectations, he tore his clothing and wept (2 Kings 22:5–13, 19). This event, in concert with Huldah's support, motivated him to read the newly discovered scriptures to the people and place them under covenant to repent and keep the Lord's commandments (see 2 Kings 23). Huldah was a major force for good and influenced Josiah and his reforms.

Some have questioned the reliability of Huldah's prophetic power because they believe she promised Josiah a peaceful death (2 Kings 22:20). He was killed in battle against Pharaoh Neco at Megiddo (2 Kings 23:29). But Huldah's prophecy refers to Josiah's being spared the horror of having to witness the terrible destruction of Jerusalem and Judah by the Babylonians, which was fulfilled. Additionally, Huldah prophesied a peaceful or honorable burial for Josiah in his own tomb, which was also fulfilled (2 Kings 23:30).

That women were called of God to hold the prophetic office at various times in history is consistent with the Lord's teachings. Alma declared that the gifts of inspiration, revelation, and prophecy are not limited to men: "And now, he imparteth his word by angels unto men, yea, not only men but women also. Now this is not all; little children do have words given unto them many times, which confound the wise and the learned" (Alma 32:23).

Of course, there is only one man on the earth at a time upon whom all the keys of the priesthood are conferred (D&C 132:7). But in both Old and New Testament times, the Lord authorized prophetesses to function alongside constituted priesthood authority. Through those priesthood administrators, ordinances were guarded and regulated and offices in God's kingdom administered. But the power and authority to disseminate the official word of the Lord was given to some women, who possessed the gift of prophecy in rich abundance. The ability to serve as conduits to heaven was their great gift. Such a gift is not limited to men, an idea that is in harmony with the doctrine of gifts described in the revelations of the Restoration (D&C 46:22).

Women possessing such gifts and powers always point us to Jesus Christ. As we know, the testimony of Jesus is the spirit of prophecy (Revelation 19:10). When the ancient Israelites followed the words of the prophetesses, they were blessed. We must likewise follow the order of the kingdom of God in our day if we want to be blessed. We would also be wise to follow the modern-day Huldahs in our lives, who help us repent and point us to Christ.

CHAPTER 15

LESSONS FROM THE PAST

Many prophets lived on the earth from the days of Adam to the meridian of time. Sacred writ is crystal clear that all of them testified of the Messiah, the Anointed One, who came to earth as Jesus of Nazareth. Abinadi said:

"For behold, did not Moses prophesy unto them concerning the coming of the Messiah, and that God should redeem his people? Yea, and even *all the prophets who have prophesied ever since the world began*—have they not spoken more or less concerning these things? Have they not said that God himself should come down among the children of men, and take upon him the form of man, and go forth in mighty power upon the face of the earth? Yea, and have they not said also that he should bring to pass the resurrection of the dead, and that he, himself, should be oppressed and afflicted?" (Mosiah 13:33–35; emphasis added).

The words of Peter are no less impressive: "The word which God sent unto the children of Israel, preaching peace by Jesus Christ: (he is Lord of all:). . . . Him God raised up the third day, and shewed him openly. . . . And he commanded us to preach unto the people, and to testify that it is he which was ordained of God to be the Judge of quick and dead. To him give all the prophets witness, that through his name whosoever believeth in him shall receive remission of sins" (Acts 10:36–43).

Even Jewish rabbinical writings of Peter's day and beyond proclaim that "all of the prophets prophesied only concerning the days of the Messiah."[1] Many of the rabbis and Jewish leaders did not recognize their Messiah-King as he walked the dusty roads of Galilee and Judea. But the prophecies of the prophets and seers are catalogued in the Hebrew Bible, our Old Testament, the human family's first testament of Jesus Christ, and those prophecies are sure and clear.

Many of the prophets foretold Christ's coming as they lived lives and lived in circumstances that paralleled, modeled, foreshadowed, and typified the life and message of Jesus the Messiah. Elder Bruce R. McConkie taught, "There are many events in the lives of many prophets that set those righteous persons apart as types and shadows of their Messiah."[2] We have examined the lives of a few of these prophets, and we have also looked at some priests and kings who, in their anointed roles and anointed stewardships, have pointed to *the* Anointed One.

Many other human types and shadows of the Messiah could be added to our discussion. One is Jonah, whose three days and nights in the belly of the whale specifically prefigured the Messiah's death, burial, and sojourn in the spirit world and whose preaching paralleled the preaching of the Messiah. Jesus' own witness points us to Jonah as a similitude:

"Then certain of the scribes and of the Pharisees answered, saying, Master, we would see a sign from thee. But he answered and said unto them, An evil and adulterous generation seeketh after a sign; and there shall no sign be given to it, but the sign of the prophet Jonas: For as Jonas was three days and three nights in the whale's belly; so shall the Son of man be three days and three nights in the heart of the earth. The men of Nineveh shall rise in judgment with this generation, and shall condemn it: because they repented at the preaching of Jonas; and behold, a greater than Jonas is here" (Matthew 12:38–41).

Not incidentally, Jonah's name means "dove," a symbol of Jesus' identity as Messiah and Son of God given at his baptism (Matthew 3:16–17).

Similarly, Jonathan, the son of Saul, was like Jesus a son of a king and one who loved the future King David (1 Samuel 13–23). Jonathan's name means "gift of Jehovah or God" and points us to Jesus, who is our gift from God. Jonathan willingly risked his life for David—one of the most unselfish attitudes in all the Old Testament, considering that David could naturally have been regarded as Jonathan's rival (1 Samuel 18:1–4). Jonathan's attitude recalls both the work and actions of Jesus, who not only taught the principle that greater love hath no man than that he lay down his life for his friends (John 15:13) but actually demonstrated it.

Another similitude of Jesus Christ is the prophet Hosea, the meaning of whose name points us to the whole mission and message of Jesus—"salvation" or "he saves." Hosea lived in the tragic final days of the Northern Kingdom of Israel. He was commanded to marry an adulterous woman, Gomer, who symbolized covenant Israel of that day. Hosea himself symbolized the Lord—his forgiving nature and his continuing relationship with Israel even though Israel had committed spiritual adultery. This story meshes with Jesus' typology of the Church as the bride and himself, Christ, as the Bridegroom (Matthew 9:15; John 3:29); compare Revelation 21:2, 9; D&C 33:17; 65:3; 88:2).

Rulers such as Josiah and Nehemiah were types and similitudes of Jesus in important ways. Josiah ("Jehovah supports or sustains") was a restorer-king, who was killed as a young man by Gentiles while trying to save Israel. Nehemiah ("Jehovah comforts" or "Jehovah is comfort") was a prophetic governor of Judea who rebuilt Jerusalem and her walls, much as the future Messiah will rebuild Jerusalem at the last day.

Indeed, much more might be said. But the examples we have discussed substantiate the claim of scripture that all things given of God testify of the Son of God, the Messiah, and are a typifying of him. The most poignant and powerful types and symbols of Christ are the people we encounter in the pages of the Old Testament—the prophets, priests, and kings we read about in the first testament of Jesus Christ. They point us to him who is the embodiment of every good deed, every righteous thought, every foreordained action that we see in the lives of the prophets, priests, and kings in ancient Israel. Thus, Jesus is the Second Adam, the actual King of Righteousness (Melchizedek), the New Moses, the Son of David, the return of Elijah, or Jeremiah, or any of the other prophets. In sum, Jesus is the Prophet, Priest, and King of our profession (Hebrews 3:1). He is the Messiah of the Old Testament and the Christ of the New.

Our challenge is to take the lessons taught in the ancient written testimonies and use them to become more Christlike—more like the Messiah to whom all of the prophets looked and of whom they spoke. Perhaps the greatest lesson on types and similitudes is the one which some of us find the most difficult to accept, but by not accepting it, we rob ourselves of the true picture of our own relationship and similarity to God: We too are similitudes of the Messiah.

All persons who take upon themselves the name of Christ are a similitude of Christ. Every person who is baptized as Christ was baptized is a similitude of Christ. Every man who holds the Melchizedek Priesthood "is or should be a type of Christ," said Elder Bruce R. McConkie. "Those who lived before he came were types and shadows and witnesses of his coming. Those who have lived since he came are witnesses of such coming and are types and shadows of what he was."[3] In short, every person who is washed, anointed, and ordained in the name of Christ, every person who immerses himself or herself in living the gospel of Christ, every person who is a witness of Christ—all these are living, walking, breathing similitudes of the Lord Jesus Christ.

What is even more startling is that the Lord has told us that the celestial kingdom will be populated with similitudes of Jesus Christ. President Joseph F. Smith recorded:

"As I pondered over these things which are written, the eyes of my understanding were opened, and the Spirit of the Lord rested upon me, and I saw the hosts of the dead, both small and great.

"And there were gathered together in one place an innumerable company of the spirits of the just, who had been faithful in the testimony of Jesus while they lived in mortality;

"And who had offered sacrifice in the similitude of the great sacrifice of the Son of God, and had suffered tribulation in their Redeemer's name" (D&C 138:11–13).

We know that we need Christ. We know that we must find Christ. We know that we must come unto Christ. But we also know that we must someday become like Christ. The first place we can find Christ is in the Old Testament—the foundation of all the other testaments of Christ. We can take a step closer to finding Christ by studying those who were similitudes of him. And we can take a step closer to becoming more like him by learning the lessons of those whose lives elucidate his life more completely. This is the great value of the Old Testament. This is the great gift that it gives to us.

NOTES

CHAPTER 1

THE FIRST TESTAMENT OF JESUS CHRIST

1. Hinckley, "Inspirational Thoughts," 3.
2. *Pirqe Avot,* 2:8.
3. Kent P. Jackson, "All Things Point to Christ," in *Studies in Scripture,* 4:1.
4. Buttrick, *Interpreter's Dictionary of the Bible,* 4:21.
5. In Robert L. Millet, "Influence of the Brass Plates," in Nyman and Tate, *Second Nephi,* 208–9.
6. McConkie, *New Witness for the Articles of Faith,* 391–92.
7. McConkie, *Promised Messiah,* 453.
8. See Skinner, *Gethsemane,* 77–91.
9. "I Know That My Redeemer Lives," *Hymns,* no. 136; emphasis added.
10. Hunter, *Church News,* 11 June 1994, 3.

CHAPTER 2

ADAM:
OUR FIRST FATHER

1. Smith, *Teachings of the Prophet Joseph Smith,* 172.
2. Ibid., 157.
3. *Webster's New World Dictionary,* s.v. "Contrite."
4. Talmage, *Jesus the Christ,* 669.
5. Christofferson, Conference Report, October 2000, 8.
6. Hinckley, "Speaking Today," 73.

CHAPTER 3

ABEL, ENOCH, AND NOAH:
OTHER FATHERS

1. Smith, *Teachings of the Prophet Joseph Smith*, 58.
2. Smith, *History of the Church*, 3:386.
3. Smith, *Teachings of the Prophet Joseph Smith*, 157.
4. Smith, *History of the Church*, 3:386; *Teachings of the Prophet Joseph Smith*, 157.

CHAPTER 4

MELCHIZEDEK:
KING OF RIGHTEOUSNESS

1. Smith, *Teachings of the Prophet Joseph Smith*, 322.
2. McConkie, *Promised Messiah*, 450.
3. Galbraith, Ogden, and Skinner, *Jerusalem*, 26–35.
4. McConkie, *Promised Messiah*, 27–28.
5. Smith, *Teachings of the Prophet Joseph Smith*, 308.
6. Josephus, *Wars of the Jews*, 6.10.1.
7. McConkie, *Promised Messiah*, 384.
8. Ibid.

CHAPTER 5

ABRAHAM, ISAAC, AND JACOB:
FATHERS OF THE FAITHFUL

1. Ballard, "Sacramental Covenant," 1029.
2. Kimball, "Example of Abraham," 4.
3. Burton, *God's Greatest Gift*, 100.
4. Ibid.
5. Smith, *Lectures on Faith*, 5:2; emphasis added.
6. Maxwell, *All These Things Shall Give Thee Experience*, 31.
7. Cannon, *Gospel Truth*, 89.
8. See Smith, *Teachings of the Prophet Joseph Smith*, 150.

CHAPTER 6

JOSEPH OF EGYPT:
THE FIRST OF MANY

1. Wilson, *Old Testament Word Studies*, 82.
2. See LDS Bible Dictionary, s.v. "Birthright," 625.
3. Talmage, *Jesus the Christ*, 592.
4. Packer, Conference Report, April 1988, 80.

NOTES

CHAPTER 7

MOSES AND JOSHUA:
LAWGIVERS AND DELIVERERS

1. McConkie, *Promised Messiah*, 442–43.
2. For a fuller treatment of the serpent as a symbol of Deity in the ancient world and its usurpation by Satan, see my "Serpent Symbols and Salvation in the Ancient Near East and the Book of Mormon," 42–55.
3. McConkie, *Promised Messiah*, 445–46.

CHAPTER 8

BOAZ AND SAMUEL:
TYPES AND SHADOWS IN THE REIGN OF THE JUDGES

1. Smith, *Teachings of the Prophet Joseph Smith Smith*, 181.
2. Ehat and Cook, *Words of Joseph Smith*, 235; spelling and punctuation standardized.
3. David Rolph Seely, "Samuel: Prophet, Priest, Judge, and Anointer of Kings," in *Studies in Scripture*, 3:271.
4. Ibid., 3:275.

CHAPTER 9

DAVID AND SOLOMON:
FATHERS OF THE ROYAL LINE

1. LDS Bible Dictionary, s.v. "David," 654.
2. *Eerdmans Dictionary of the Bible*, 822.
3. McConkie, *Promised Messiah*, 188.
4. Ibid., 190.
5. *Interpreter's Bible*, 7:250.
6. McConkie, *Promised Messiah*, 188.
7. *Interpreter's Bible*, 7:527.
8. Talmage, *Jesus the Christ*, 517.

CHAPTER 10

ELIJAH AND ELISHA:
POWER OVER THE ELEMENTS

1. McConkie, *Mormon Doctrine*, 222.
2. LDS Bible Dictionary, s.v. "Elisha," 664.
3. Clark, Conference Report, April 1951, 78.
4. McConkie, "Ten Blessings of the Priesthood," in *Priesthood*, 33.
5. McConkie, *Doctrinal New Testament Commentary*, 1:162.
6. Ibid., 1:256.

CHAPTER 11

HEZEKIAH:
DELIVERER OF JERUSALEM

1. Petersen, *Isaiah for Today,* 14.

CHAPTER 12

ISAIAH AND JEREMIAH:
SIMILITUDES DURING IMPENDING DOOM

1. LDS Bible Dictionary, s.v. "Isaiah," 707, and "Jeremiah," 711.
2. Parry, Parry, and Petersen, *Understanding Isaiah,* 72–73.
3. Ibid., 81–82.
4. Jeff Chadwick, correspondence, May 2005.
5. Smith, *Teachings of the Prophet Joseph Smith,* 181.
6. For a fuller treatment, see Welch and Hall, *Charting the New Testament,* 10–16.

CHAPTER 13

CYRUS:
A UNIQUE MESSIAH

1. Pritchard, *Ancient Near Eastern Texts,* 316.
2. Smith, *History of the Church,* 4:257.
3. Josephus, *Antiquities of the Jews,* 11.1.1–2.
4. Anderson, *Understanding the Old Testament,* 508–9.
5. Pritchard, *Ancient Near Eastern Texts,* 315–16.
6. Benson, "Civic Standards for the Faithful Saints," 59.

CHAPTER 14

ESTHER, DEBORAH, AND HULDAH:
WOMEN OF POWER AND MESSIANIC PORTENT

1. *Interpreter's Bible,* 3:837.
2. Josephus, *Antiquities of the Jews,* 11.6.1.
3. Ibid., 11.6.2.
4. *Interpreter's Bible,* 3:848.
5. Ibid., 3:843.

CHAPTER 15

LESSONS FROM THE PAST

1. Neusner, *Tractate Sanhedrin,* 23C:141.
2. McConkie, *Promised Messiah,* 453.
3. Ibid., 451.

SOURCES

Ancient Near Eastern Texts Relating to the Old Testament. Edited by
   James B. Pritchard. Princeton, N.J.: Princeton University Press,
   1969.

Anderson, Bernard W. *Understanding the Old Testament.* Englewood
   Cliffs, N.J.: Prentice-Hall, 1966.

Ballard, Melvin J. "The Sacramental Covenant." *Improvement Era,*
   October 1919, 1029.

Benson, Ezra Taft. "Civic Standards for the Faithful Saints." *Ensign,*
   July 1972, 59.

Burton, Theodore M. *God's Greatest Gift.* Salt Lake City: Deseret
   Book, 1977.

Cannon, George Q. *Gospel Truth.* Edited by Jerreld L. Newquist. 2
   vols. in 1. Salt Lake City: Deseret Book, 1987.

Christofferson, D. Todd. Conference Report, October 2000, 8.

Conference Report. Salt Lake City: The Church of Jesus Christ of
   Latter-day Saints, 1951, 1988, 2000.

Eerdmans Dictionary of the Bible. Edited by David Noel Freeman.
   Grand Rapids, Mich.: Eerdmans, 2000.

Ehat, Andrew F., and Lyndon W. Cook, comps. and eds. *The Words
   of Joseph Smith.* Orem, Utah: Grandin Book, 1991.

Galbraith, David B., D. Kelly Ogden, and Andrew C. Skinner.
   Jerusalem, the Eternal City. Salt Lake City: Deseret Book, 1996.

Hinckley, Gordon B. "Inspirational Thoughts." *Ensign,* August 1997, 3.

———. "Speaking Today: Excerpts from Recent Addresses of President Gordon B. Hinckley." *Ensign,* January 1998, 73.

Hunter, Howard W. *Church News,* 11 June 1994, 3.

Hymns of The Church of Jesus Christ of Latter-day Saints. Salt Lake City: The Church of Jesus Christ of Latter-day Saints, 1985.

The Interpreter's Bible. 12 vols. Nashville, Tenn.: Abingdon, 1951.

The Interpreter's Dictionary of the Bible. Edited by George A. Buttrick. Nashville, Tenn.: Abingdon Press, 1962.

Jackson, Kent P., and Robert L. Millet, eds. 8 vols. Salt Lake City: Deseret Book, 2004.

Josephus, Flavius. *The Antiquities of the Jews* and *Wars of the Jews.* In *Josephus: Complete Works.* Translated by William Whiston. Grand Rapids, Mich.: Kregel Publications, 1960.

Kimball, Spencer W. "The Example of Abraham." *Ensign,* June 1975, 4.

Maxwell, Neal A. *All These Things Shall Give Thee Experience.* Salt Lake City: Deseret Book, 1980.

McConkie, Bruce R. *Doctrinal New Testament Commentary.* 3 vols. Salt Lake City: Bookcraft, 1965–73.

———. *The Promised Messiah.* Salt Lake City: Deseret Book, 1978.

———. *A New Witness for the Articles of Faith.* Salt Lake City: Deseret Book, 1985.

———. *Mormon Doctrine.* 2d ed. Salt Lake City: Bookcraft, 1966.

Nyman, Monte S., and Charles D. Tate Jr., eds. *Second Nephi: The Doctrinal Structure.* Provo, Utah: Religious Studies Center, Brigham Young University, 1989.

Packer, Boyd K. Conference Report, April 1988, 80.

Parry, Donald W., Jay A. Parry, and Tina M. Peterson. *Understanding Isaiah.* Salt Lake City: Deseret Book, 1998.

Petersen, Mark E. *Isaiah for Today.* Salt Lake City: Deseret Book, 1981.

Priesthood. Salt Lake City: Deseret Book, 1981.

Skinner, Andrew C. *Gethsemane.* Salt Lake City: Deseret Book, 2002.

———. "Serpent Symbols and Salvation in the Ancient Near East and the Book of Mormon." *Journal of Book of Mormon Studies* 10, no. 2 (2001).

Smith, Joseph. *History of The Church of Jesus Christ of Latter-day Saints.* Edited by B. H. Roberts. 2d ed. rev. 7 vols. Salt Lake City: The Church of Jesus Christ of Latter-day Saints, 1932–51.

———. *Lectures on Faith.* Salt Lake City: Deseret Book, 1999.

———. *Teachings of the Prophet Joseph Smith.* Selected by Joseph Fielding Smith. Salt Lake City: Deseret Book, 1976.

Talmage, James E. *Jesus the Christ.* 3d ed. Salt Lake City: Deseret Book, 1916.

The Words of Joseph Smith. Compiled and edited by Andrew F. Ehat and Lyndon W. Cook. Orem, Utah: Grandin Book, 1991.

Welch, John W., and John F. Hall. *Charting the New Testament.* Provo, Utah: Foundation for Ancient Research and Mormon Studies (FARMS), 2002.

Wilson, William. *Old Testament Word Studies.* Grand Rapids, Mich.: Kregel Publications, 1978.

INDEX

Abel: a profound similitude of Jesus Christ, 15, 17, 18; mistakenly identified as Messiah, 18–20

Abinadi, testifies of Jesus Christ, 133

Abraham: commanded to sacrifice son, 35; exemplar of consecration, 38; a dual similitude of Heavenly Father and Jesus Christ, 39–41, 42

Abrahamic covenant, 35, 44

Adam, 9; foreshadows Jesus Christ, 10–12; held keys of First Presidency, 11

Ahaz, king, 102

Alma (Book of Mormon prophet): on Melchizedek, 27–28; on Liahona, 63–64; on gifts of inspiration, 131

Altar: meaning of word, 37; as metaphor for consecrating possessions, 38

Anointing, in ancient Israel, 7–8

Atonement: all things center on, 1; gives life after physical death, 10; broken heart and contrite spirit symbolize, 13

Ballard, Melvin J.: on similitude of Abraham's sacrifice, 34–45

Bethlehem, meaning of word, 65

Benson, Ezra Taft: on Cyrus's role in the Lord's plan, 116–17

Birthright, blessings of, 46–47

Boaz: a similitude of Jesus Christ, 67, 69; marries Ruth, 67–68; a redeemer, 68–69

Book of Mormon: doctrine of, 4–5; another testament of Jesus Christ, 5

Brass plates: as version of Old Testament, 4–5; contained messianic testimonies, 5

Brass serpent, as similitude of Jesus Christ, 58–59

Brother of Jared, on the Fall, 9

Burton, Theodore M., on obedience of Abraham, 37

Cain: made covenant with Satan, 17; represents Satan, 19–20

and purpose of Old Testament,
6; on prophets as types and
shadows of Jesus Christ, 7, 134;
on ordinances as types of Jesus
Christ, 27; on sacrament of the
Lord's Supper, 31; on likeness
of Moses and Jesus Christ,
55–56, 61; on Messiah's
lineage, 78, 79; on priesthood
power, 85; on similitude of
Elijah and Elisha, 86; on being
a similitude of Jesus Christ,
137

Melchizedek: meaning of name,
25; titles and designations
point to Jesus Christ, 25; stood
in Lord's place, 26; effected
changes among people, 27–28,
31; a similitude of Messiah, 31

Melchizedek Priesthood, 26

Messiah: meaning of word, 7; to
be son of David, 79; Pharisees'
understanding of, 79–80

Moroni, declares people to be
remnant of Joseph, 52

Mortality, greatest lessons of, 41

Moses: a similitude of Jesus Christ,
55, 56–57, 60–61; possessed
spirit of prophecy, 57; made
serpent of brass as similitude of
Jesus Christ, 58–59; a second
witness of Jesus Christ, 61

Mount Moriah, site of Abraham's
sacrifice, 39

Mount Nebo, site of Moses' final
prophecies, 57

Mount Zion, becoming saviors on,
14

Naaman, Syrian general healed by
Elisha, 86–87

Nativity, foreshadowed by
Samuel's birth, 70–72

Nehemiah, a similitude of Jesus
Christ, 136

Nephi: delights in testifying of
Christ, 6–7; slays Laban,
127–28

New Testament: documents
fulfillment of ancient laws and
promises, 4

Noah: ordained at young age, 22;
a similitude of Jesus Christ, 23;
as Gabriel, 23

Obedience: example of Adam's,
10; to priesthood ordinances,
29

Old Testament: principal witness
of Jesus Christ, 2–3, 6, 8;
contains laws and promises of
ancient Israel, 3–4; foundation
of Book of Mormon, 4–5;
elements of, 6; contains types
and shadows of Jesus Christ, 7;
first testament of Jesus Christ,
134, 137

Ordinances, purpose of, 29–30

Paul: on similitude of Jesus Christ
and Adam, 10; on Melchizedek
as a type of Jesus Christ, 26; on
baptism, 29; on Abraham's
sacrifice, 36

Peter, testifies of Jesus Christ,
133–34

Pharisees, 79–80

Pratt, Parley P.: on similarities of
Joseph Smith and Cyrus, 116

Priesthood, sacrificial offerings a
duty of, 11

Priesthood holders: symbolize
Jesus Christ when officiating in
saving ordinances, 13–14; will
have power to govern all things,

PROPHETS,
PRIESTS,
AND KINGS